Rhythm & Blues You Can Use

A COMPLETE GUIDE TO LEARNING R&B, SOUL, AND FUNK GUITAR STYLES

BY JOHN GANAPES

ISBN 978-1-4234-9653-3

HAL•LEONARD® CORPORATION

7777 W. BLUEMOUND RD. P.O. BOX 13819 MILWAUKEE, WI 53213

In Australia Contact:
Hal Leonard Australia Pty. Ltd.
4 Lentara Court
Cheltenham, Victoria, 3192 Australia
Email: ausadmin@halleonard.com.au

Visit Hal Leonard Online at
www.halleonard.com

ACKNOWLEDGMENTS

This book is dedicated to my girls, Alexandra and Sophia, and to my wife, Kathleen. Never a day goes by in which I am not deeply touched by them. And to my Tai Chi masters, sifu Ray Hayward and sifu Paul Abdella. They have taught me how to be both disciplined and relaxed.

I also want to thank Matthew Zimmerman from Wild Sound Studios in Minneapolis for again making the recording process relaxed, easy, and fun. And thanks to David D.T. Harris and Nick Zwack for working and rehearsing with me to make the music tight and grooving. Matthew, D.T., Nick, and I recorded 36 tracks in just under eight hours! I couldn't have done it without their talents.

TABLE OF CONTENTS

All music composed and arranged by John Ganapes
Produced by John Ganapes with Matthew Zimmerman
Recorded at Wild Sound Studio, Minneapolis, MN
Engineer: Matthew Zimmerman

Musicians:
John Ganapes—Guitars
David D.T. Harris—Bass
Nicholas Zwack—Drums

HOW TO USE THIS BOOK

Who Can Use This Book

This book was designed for you if:

- You have achieved at least an intermediate level of guitar proficiency, you are able to finger chords fairly well (you'll improve with this book), and you know the basic blues scales. (If you have completed *Blues You Can Use*, the first book in this series, you are at the proper level.)

- You know some blues techniques and styles, but want to learn the great R&B licks and tricks used in soul and rhythm & blues tunes, as well as in crossover rock tunes like those performed by Jimi Hendrix and Stevie Ray Vaughan.

- You want to expand your knowledge of chords and chord theory and your ability to use them in many types of settings.

- You teach and would like to have an organized set of lessons to teach R&B guitar styles to your students.

How Much Time to Spend on Each Lesson

Take your time with the lessons. Each lesson contains a lot of information. Be sure you understand the material before moving on. You can easily spend two or three weeks on each one. Depending on your current level of knowledge and ability, you may move through the lessons at a faster rate. You also could take more time on them. The Scale and Chord sections of the lessons build upon each other, so it is important to take in everything before moving on.

The Format of the Book

Each lesson is divided into four parts: Scales, Chords, Rhythm Guitar Styles, and Lead Guitar Styles. The main thrust of this book is to teach you how to build chords, how to use them and play them over the entire fingerboard, and how to use them as a reference for single-note playing. Because the lessons of the book build upon each other, you will receive maximum benefit by following *Rhythm & Blues You Can Use* in the order in which it is presented.

The Audio Supplement

The *Rhythm & Blues You Can Use* audio CD contains all of the studies, both the rhythm guitar and the lead guitar parts, in this book. The audio is played with a full band backing. The studies are played twice: once at a slow tempo, and once at full tempo.

On both the slow- and the full-tempo versions, the rhythm guitar parts are more prominent in the left channel, and the lead guitar parts are prominent in the right channel.

Each tune begins with a click of the beat so you can accurately start with the music. Tuning notes are presented on the first track. Be sure to tune to them so you are in tune with the recording.

Notes on the Notation

All of the studies are presented both in standard music notation and in tablature, as is customary in contemporary guitar study. Due to the complexity of this book's repeat patterns, a brief explanation is in order:

> **D.C. al Coda** means to go back to the top (beginning) of the tune and play until you come to the **To Coda** ⊕ instruction. From there, you skip to the ⊕ **Coda** section (i.e., the ending section).

> **D.S. al Coda** means to go back to the ⅀ symbol, which will be located at an earlier section in the score, and play until you come to the **To Coda** ⊕ instruction. From there, you skip to the ⊕ **Coda** section.

If you follow along in the score as you listen to the recording, these repeats should become clear.

Practice

In general, the more you practice, the faster you will learn. That said, it's important to understand that daily practice is much more beneficial than one "marathon" session per week. You should aim for five days (or more) per week—every week—even if for only 15 or 20 minutes some days.

As you work through the material in the Scales and Chords sections of the lessons, it is most often best to use the Circle of 4ths, as presented below, while working through all of the keys. The first two or three keys—C major and F major, for example—are presented, but you are expected to continue through the rest. Thus, you would start with the key of C major (at the top of the circle) and move clockwise through F, B♭, E♭, and so on, all the way around to G.

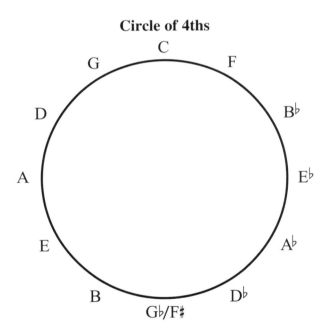

Note: The terms "bar" and "measure" are interchangeable and refer to the unit of beat groupings—like four beats in a bar of 4/4 or 12 beats in a bar of 12/8, etc. The practice in this book is to use "bar" when referring to "the fourth bar in the tune" or "there are eight bars in the tune," and to use "measure" when labeling a measure/bar, such as "measure 3" or "measure 12."

Rhythm & Blues You Can Use—Online!

You will find bonus material and music, hints, techniques, and other supplements for this book at *bluesyoucanuse.com*. Visit the site to connect with fellow students, as well. For video clips of the masters, "Like" *Blues You Can Use* on Facebook.

In this first lesson, we'll look at a simple I–IV chord progression and mix the pentatonic scales with their associated chords, both in the rhythm guitar part and the lead guitar part. This study has a very simple form. *Form* is the overall scheme, or structure, of a piece of music, including the number of sections (parts) it contains, the length of the sections (total bars), and the melodic and harmonic (chord) themes of each section.

This study is an eight-bar, two-chord vamp, with a small change at the end. A *vamp* is a short chordal or rhythmic phrase that is repeated. A vamp can be used as an intro, as a setting over which to improvise, or as the whole structure of a tune.

THE SCALES

Rhythm & blues lead guitar lines are very often derived from *major pentatonic scales*, which you should know pretty well by now. They are covered thoroughly in Lessons 12–14 of *Blues You Can Use*.

To use major pentatonic scales effectively, you must be able to get around on them with ease. You also have to see the major chords from which they are built. There is a different major chord embedded within each of the five patterns. Look at the following diagrams, presented here separately, as well as combined along the fretboard.

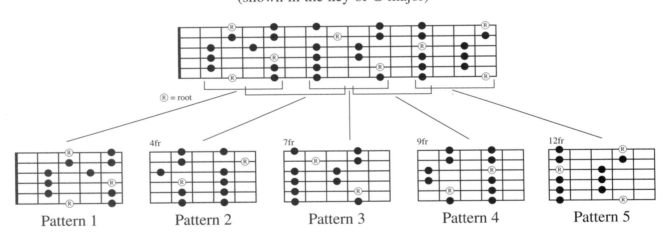

Major Pentatonic Scale Along the Fingerboard
(shown in the key of G major)

Pattern 1   Pattern 2   Pattern 3   Pattern 4   Pattern 5

You should already have a handle on them, having studied them in *Blues You Can Use* or elsewhere. Here, we will focus on the chord-scale relationships. Together, they form a chord/scale. A *chord/scale* is constructed of the notes of a chord, combined with the notes of a related, corresponding scale.

We'll look at the chords/scales individually. Here is the first pattern, built from Pattern 1 of the major pentatonic scale, along with its related chord—a full, sixth-string-root barre chord.

Major Pentatonic Chord/Scale Study
Pattern 1

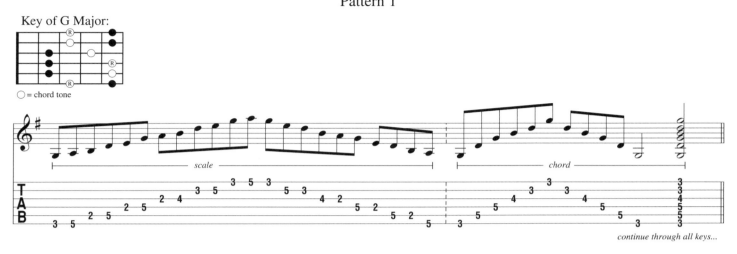

continue through all keys...

THE CHORDS

Triads are constructed of three notes and are the most basic chord types. You can arrange the notes in any order and/or double some (or all) of the notes, but the chord remains the same.

There are four types of triads: major, minor, diminished, and augmented. We'll look at only the first two types, since they are, by far, the most commonly used triads.

The three notes of a triad are the root, 3rd, and 5th. The *root* contains the same letter name as the chord—G major has a G note for a root; C minor has a C note for its root.

The *3rd* makes the quality of the chord either major or minor. If you lower the 3rd by one half step, or one fret, the quality of the chord becomes minor. The *5th* fills out the chord. We call the root, 3rd, and 5th the "1, 3, and 5" of the chord, respectively.

The root doesn't need to be the bottom note. As mentioned earlier, you can put the notes in any order. If the root is *not* the bottom note, the chord is inverted. An *inverted chord* contains a note other than the root in the bass (bottom).

It's useful to know the basic inversions, both for your lead playing and for your rhythm playing. Here are some commonly used inversions, with the notes of the chord labeled. Although there are many, many voicings for any given chord, here I'll limit the number to those found on the top four strings.

Simple Three-Note Triads

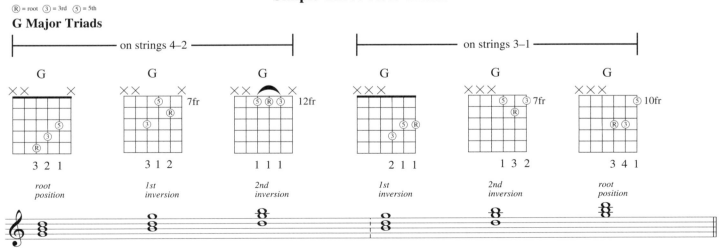

G Minor Triads

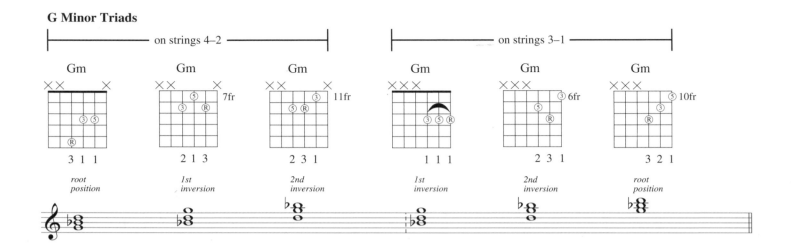

Four-Note Triads with Doubling

G Major Triads

G Minor Triads

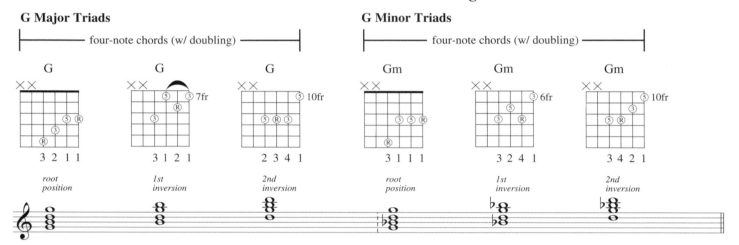

Once you have become familiar with the individual voicings, you need to study how they are arranged on the fingerboard relative to each other. Below, the major triads, built on strings 4–2, and their inversions are illustrated. The major triads are presented in a I–IV progression, like the one in "Easy Rhythm," the study from this lesson. Practice the triads in all 12 keys, through the Circle of 4ths. (Minor triads will be presented later in the book.)

(This has been an extremely brief explanation of chord theory. For a more thorough explanation, see my *Blues You Can Use: Guitar Chords* book.)

Major Triad Inversions in a I–IV Progression
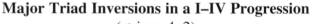
(strings 4–2)

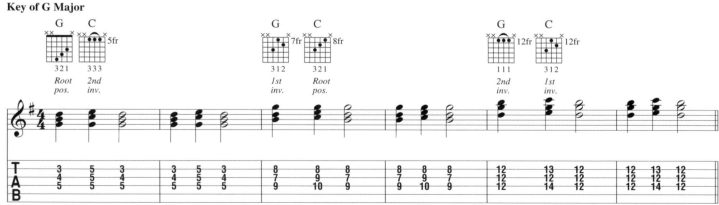

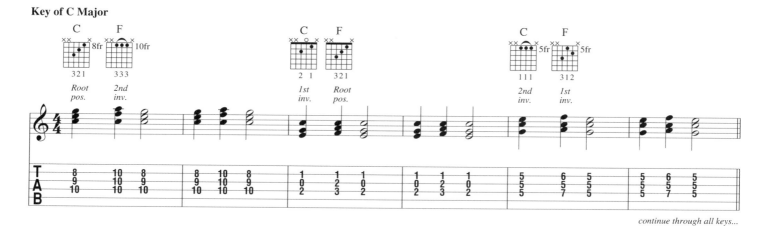

continue through all keys...

RHYTHM GUITAR STYLES

The rhythm guitar part to "Easy Rhythm," the first study in this book, is based on two simple major chords, a sixth-string-root barre chord and a fifth-string-root barre chord, and simple lead lines that are constructed from the corresponding major pentatonic chord/scale.

As you play the rhythm guitar part to "Easy Rhythm," note how the major pentatonic scale segments fit together with the chords.

TRACK 2
Slow Tempo

TRACK 3
Full Tempo

EASY RHYTHM
Rhythm

LEAD GUITAR STYLES

As you start to work on the lead guitar part to "Easy Rhythm," pay close attention to which major pentatonic scale patterns you are playing. The scale patterns follow the chord changes, so when an A chord is sounded, you use an A major pentatonic scale, and when you are on a D chord, you play a D scale.

EASY RHYTHM
Lead

TRACK 2
Slow Tempo

TRACK 3
Full Tempo

LESSON 2

In this lesson, we'll look at a simple I–IV–V chord progression and how it might be treated in an older R&B style—like something that might have been written in the early '60s. The tune is very straight-forward and easy—something that an old R&B musician friend of mine used to call "ice cream" for its simplicity and sweetness.

THE SCALES

By now, you should have a good handle on the major pentatonic chord/scale based on Pattern 1. If not, go back and practice it some more. Once you feel comfortable enough with Pattern 1, you can start practicing Pattern 2, shown below.

Major Pentatonic Chord/Scale Study
Pattern 2

continue through all keys...

THE CHORDS

In Lesson 1, you learned a I–IV chord movement, using major triads that were built on strings 4–2. Now we'll look at triads that are built on the top three strings (3–1), which are arranged in the same I–IV chord movement that was presented in Lesson 1.

Triad Inversions in a I–IV Progression
(strings 3–1)

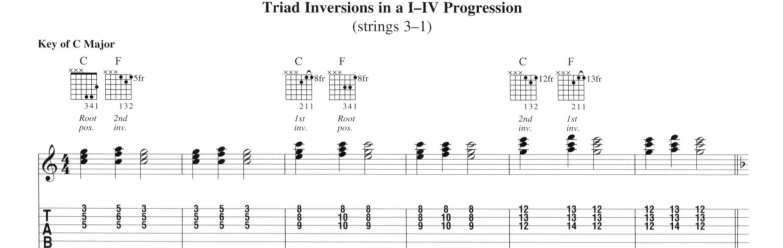

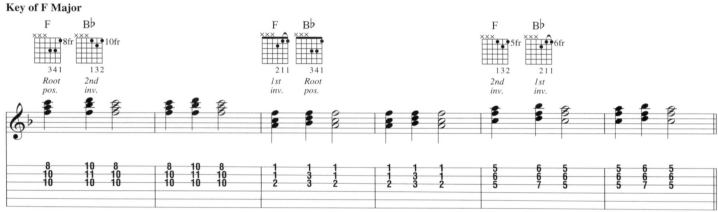

continue through all keys...

RHYTHM GUITAR STYLES

In "Lost Love," this lesson's tune, the rhythm guitar part is played with arpeggios. *Arpeggios* are chords that are played one note at a time and are often heard in R&B tunes.

An arpeggio gives the accompaniment part a sense of gentle, easy movement. Although the technique requires some cross-string picking ability, it's not difficult. Try to get a steady, flowing sound as you play the arpeggios. If you need to, play them very slowly to maintain control and keep an even rhythm. As you work through the tune, follow the picking pattern that is notated between the notation and tab staves. If you like, you can adjust the picking pattern to something more suitable for you—just be sure to be consistent.

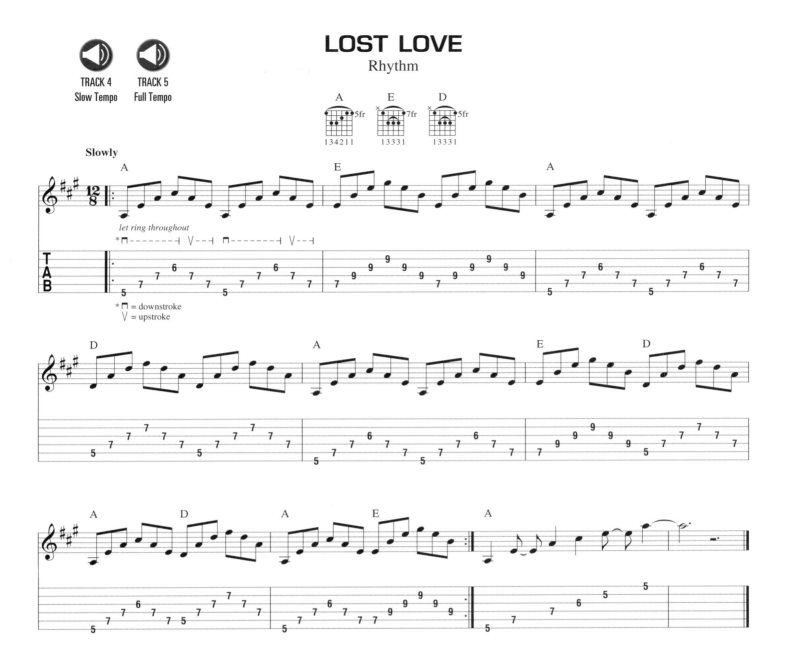

TRACK 4
Slow Tempo

TRACK 5
Full Tempo

LOST LOVE
Rhythm

The tune is written in 12/8 time, which is an easy way to notate 4/4 time with a triplet feel. That is, the four beats in a measure of 4/4 time are subdivided into three even triplets. The resulting count is:

4/4 Time: 1-&-a, 2-&-a, 3-&-a, 4-&-a

12/8 Time: 1-2-3, 4-5-6, 7-8-9, 10-11-12

In each bar, we play the arpeggios from the lowest note (on either the sixth string or the fifth string) to the highest note (on either the third string or the second string), and then back down, creating a two-beat pattern. For the I chord (A major), we start on the sixth string; for the IV and V chords (D and E), we start on the fifth string.

There is one chord presented per bar until measure 6, where the harmonic rhythm speeds up, doubling the number of chords per measure. *Harmonic rhythm* is the duration of each chord (number of beats) or how quickly or slowly the chords change.

It is very important that you hit the downbeat (first beat of each measure) precisely on time! If you waver on that note, where the chords change, the whole tune will waver rhythmically and won't groove. This is true for any beat on which a chord change occurs, though the first beat is of the utmost importance.

As you play "Lost Love," try to establish a "swaying" rhythmic feel, with the following accents: **1**-&-a, **2**-&-a, **3**-&-a, **4**-&-a. And remember, keep it steady—right now, that's more important than playing up to tempo.

LEAD GUITAR STYLES

The lead part to "Lost Love" is as simple as the rhythm part. It makes use of repeated figures (licks) that are drawn almost entirely from the major pentatonic scales relative to each of the chords—like you saw in Lesson 1. You change the scale to fit the chord, which is a soloing approach that is not used much in the blues (where you stay primarily on one scale, with notes of the chords thrown in for more color). Here, you follow the chord changes. It's more like jazz in that way.

In the solo to "Lost Love," you will notice the use of triplet figures to get sort of a flourish. Try to play them with a light touch to create an airy, floating feeling. You want to use a very light touch on the slides to achieve a smooth glide.

TRACK 4
Slow Tempo

TRACK 5
Full Tempo

LOST LOVE
Lead

LESSON 3

The chord progression in this lesson's study, "Slow Dance Dreams," is a bit deceptive. It starts out in the key of F major, with a V–I (C–F) movement. Then, in measure 5, it changes to a G major chord, moving between G and C for four bars, a V–I movement in the key of C major. Ultimately, the tune resolves to C, establishing that as the key center.

The lead part is really more like an active rhythm, something that lead guitarists frequently are called on to play in an R&B setting. This would be an ensemble accompaniment of a singer in which neither guitar part is intended to stand out.

The form of "Slow Dance Dreams" is pretty simple and common. A four-bar intro is followed by a four-bar verse, which is repeated. At the end, there is an eight-bar Coda. A *Coda* is simply an ending—a way to end a tune elegantly, or at least without being too abrupt. In Italian, Coda means "tail." (Lots of musical terms are Italian.)

The score is notated in 4/4 time, with the triplet feel that was described in Lesson 2, giving you an opportunity to see what that looks like. "Slow Dance Dreams" could just as well have been notated in 12/8 time, like "Lost Love."

THE SCALES

Continue practicing Patterns 1 and 2 of the major pentatonic chord/scale and now add Pattern 3, shown below, to your practice regimen. Remember to transpose them to every key.

Major Pentatonic Chord/Scale Study
Pattern 3

Key of G Major:

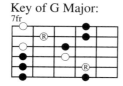

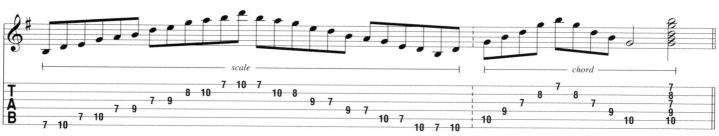

continue through all keys...

THE CHORDS

In the last two lessons, you were given three-note triads that were built on the top strings. As you saw in Lesson 1, you can double any of the notes of the triads to create a four-note chord. Those chords are presented below, in a I–IV movement.

Triad Inversions in a I–IV Progression
(four-note chords with doubling)

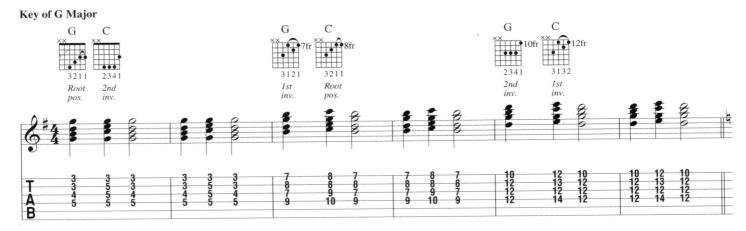

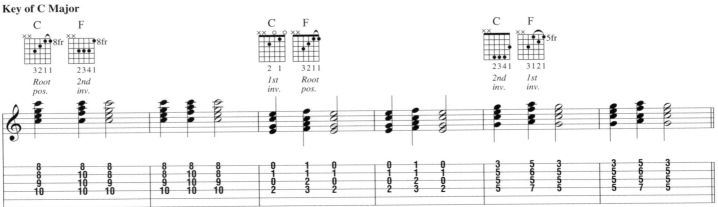

continue through all keys...

RHYTHM GUITAR STYLES

The rhythm guitar accompaniment to "Slow Dance Dreams" is arranged in an arpeggiated style, much like that in "Lost Love," the second study of this book.

SLOW DANCE DREAMS
Rhythm

TRACK 6   TRACK 7
Slow Tempo   Full Tempo

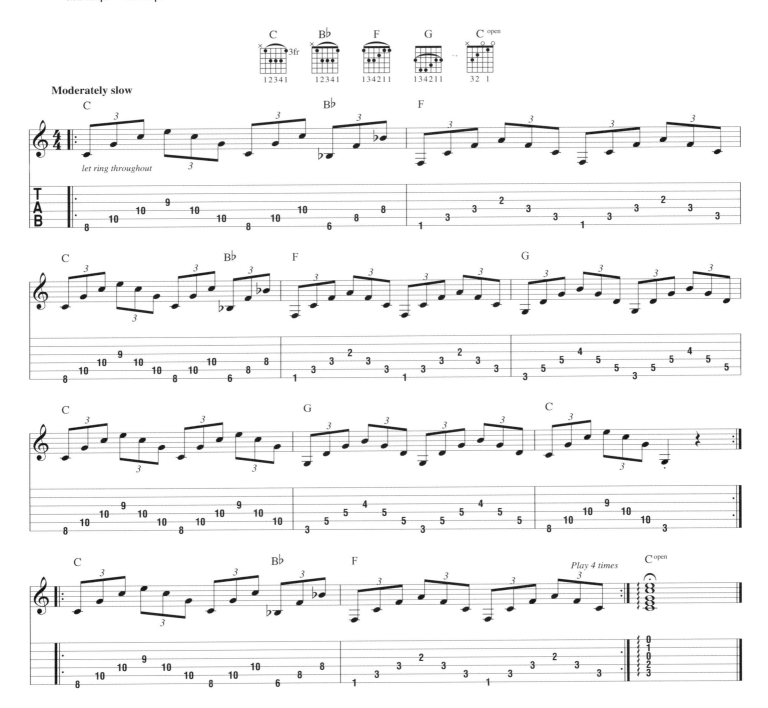

LEAD GUITAR STYLES

As I pointed out at the top of this lesson, the lead guitar part to "Slow Dance Dreams" is really an active rhythm. It makes use of the three-note triads that you learned earlier in this book.

In addition to the chords, a few single-note lines are used to lead into some of the chord changes. They are derived from the major pentatonic chord/scales that you are learning.

SLOW DANCE DREAMS
Lead

TRACK 6
Slow Tempo

TRACK 7
Full Tempo

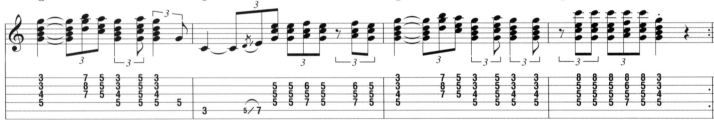

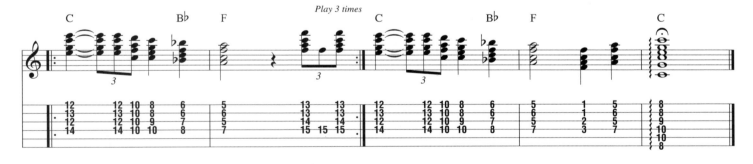

This lesson's study, "Raking in the Soul," has a Caribbean flavor. This comes from the strumming technique used in the rhythm guitar part. Early New Orleans soul and R&B artists often borrowed rhythms and techniques from the islands. Later artists discovered those ideas through those early soul and R&B musicians, including early '60s rock & rollers. There is a fine distinction between rock and R&B, and it can be difficult to discern where one leaves off and the other picks up.

THE SCALES

Here's Pattern 4 of the major pentatonic chord/scale. As you learn this pattern, continue to practice Patterns 1–3.

Major Pentatonic Chord/Scale Study
Pattern 4

Key of G Major:

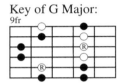

continue through all keys...

THE CHORDS

In Lesson 1, you learned that if a ♭3rd is present in a triad, the triad is minor. Here is a review of how you can make a major chord minor. Notice that the 3rd is the only note that changes (it is moved down one half step).

Changing Major Triads to Minor
(flat the 3rd)

Root Position

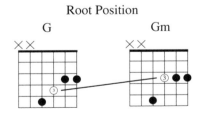

1st Inversion

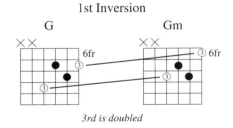

3rd is doubled

2nd Inversion

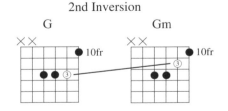

21

Here's an exercise to help you learn the previous minor chords, both three-note and four-note versions. It utilizes the same I–IV chord movement that you had in earlier lessons, only now it's minor (i–iv).

Minor Triad Inversions in a i–iv Progression

(key of G minor)

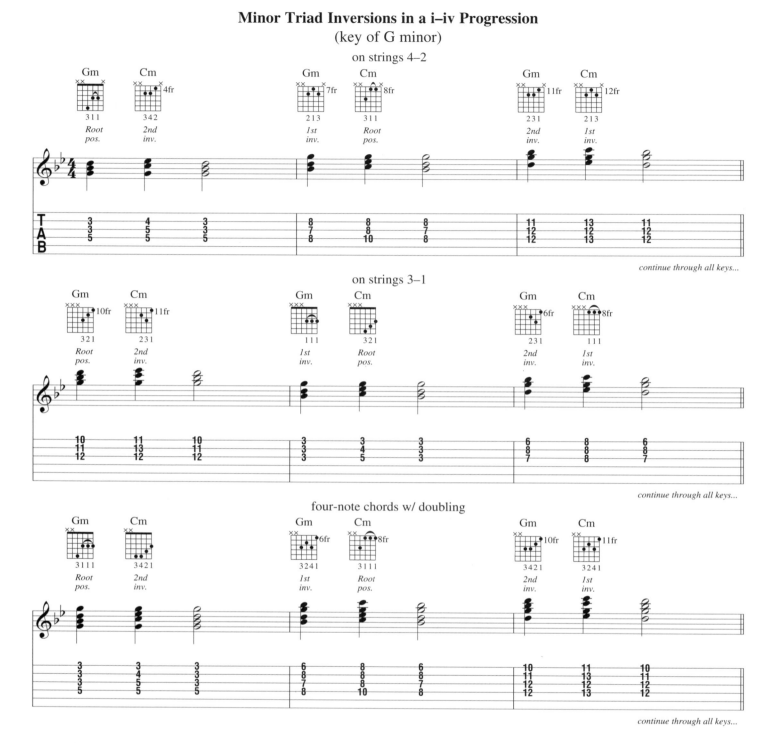

continue through all keys...

continue through all keys...

continue through all keys...

RHYTHM GUITAR STYLES

The technique used in the rhythm part to "Raking in the Soul" gives the tune its characteristic feel. The technique involves "raking" your pick across the strings on each chord change. A *string rake* is a technique whereby you quickly glide the pick across a group of consecutive strings to a target note on the last string plucked.

You start by plucking the bass (bottom) note of the chord, and then rake your pick in a downward motion from the next string to the top note of the rake (second string), which should be cut short. Lastly, play the top note of the chord (first string).

The technique is pretty clear in the score. You can practice each chord shape individually up and down the neck, fret by fret, until you get a better handle on using this technique.

The progression to "Raking in the Soul," written in C major, is constructed from the I, vi, IV, and V (C, Am, F, and G) chords of the key.

RAKING IN THE SOUL
Rhythm

LEAD GUITAR STYLES

The lead guitar part to "Raking in the Soul" is built from the pentatonic scales related to the chords. The guitar lines move and change with the chords, as you saw in the last lesson.

The C and G chord shapes themselves are used as well. You will notice that the chord and the scale shapes look very much alike, with the scale shapes containing two more notes than the chords.

As you play the lead guitar part, look for the elements that were described in the study.

RAKING IN THE SOUL

Lead

TRACK 8
Slow Tempo

TRACK 9
Full Tempo

Moderately

LESSON 5

In Lesson 5, we'll look at a '60s soul-style tune, "Sweet Soul Song." The study opens with a four-bar intro, with the chords moving up the neck from G (I chord) through B♭, C (IV chord), and on up to E♭ (♭IV chord), before moving down to D (V chord). Variations of this type of chord movement were employed in the '60s to create a big, exciting section for the song. Often, these chord movements were used in the intro, and later for the chorus or the ending.

THE SCALES

Now we are going to look at the fifth and final major pentatonic chord/scale shape, Pattern 5. At this point, you should practice all five patterns daily.

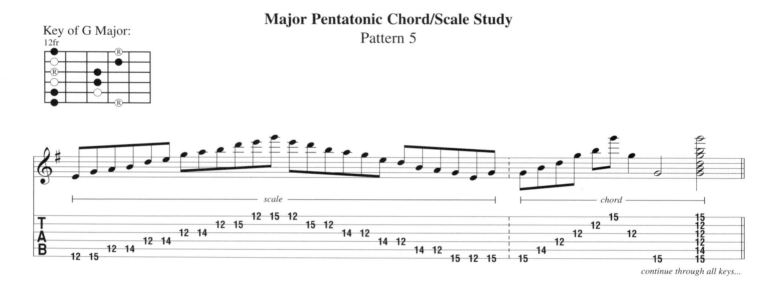

Key of G Major:

Major Pentatonic Chord/Scale Study
Pattern 5

continue through all keys...

THE CHORDS

In R&B styles, the three- and four-note chords that you learned in the previous lessons are used extensively. However, they typically are not played on the bottom (fifth and sixth) strings because they tend to sound muddy and too bassy. If the bottom strings are used, the chords are usually the bigger, five- and six-note versions, so the upper, brighter strings counteract the bassy sound of the bottom strings.

Frequently, one inversion of the smaller chord types moves to another inversion, using a passing chord to connect the two chords. A *passing chord* is a chord that is a step between two chords in a progression, played "in passing" from one chord to the next. A passing chord doesn't "count" as a chord change in and of itself.

When a passing chord is used between inversions of a I chord, a IV6 chord is employed. For example, in the key of G major, C6 (IV6) is used as the passing chord between the inversions of the G (I) chord. On the following page are some 6th chord voicings.

Sixth Chords

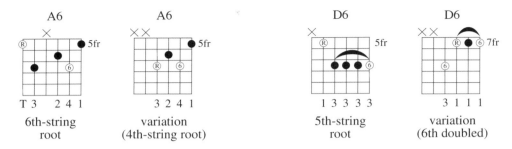

Now here are some passing IV6 chord possibilities. The following example uses smaller, three-note fragments of the larger chords from the previous example.

Major 6th Chords as Passing IV Chords

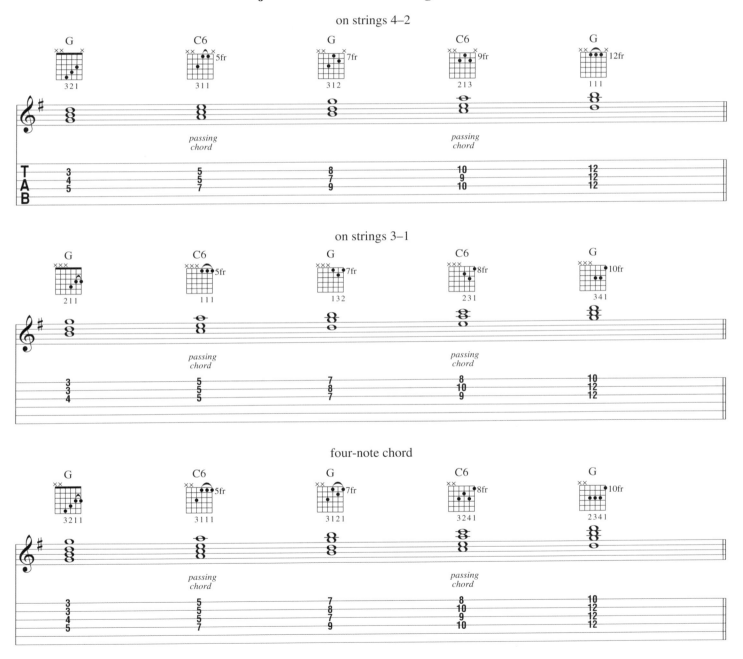

Since passing chords are such a commonly used device, you really need to get a good handle on using them. Work through all of the keys, trying to stay within the first 12 frets or so. That means that the root-position chords may be found further up the neck from the inversions. Take your time with this exercise.

RHYTHM GUITAR STYLES

The rhythm guitar part to "Sweet Soul Song" is a (very) active rhythm. You might think it's the lead guitar part, and it could be. Hopefully, you are beginning to notice that when both guitarists are in an accompaniment role, their parts may resemble each other. What you learn for rhythm guitar can be used in a lead part, and vice versa. There's not always a clear distinction.

After the intro, where simple block chords are used, the rhythm becomes active. *Block chords* are those which move from one full, solid shape to the next solid shape. You strum the whole chord, with no "ornaments."

In the following rhythm part, note embellishments from the major pentatonic chord/scales, which you already have learned, are used.

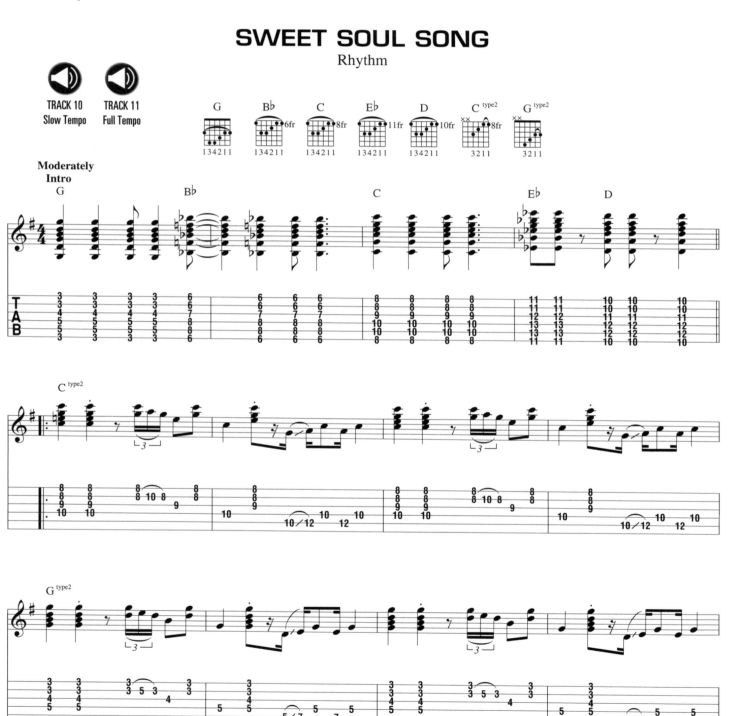

SWEET SOUL SONG
Rhythm

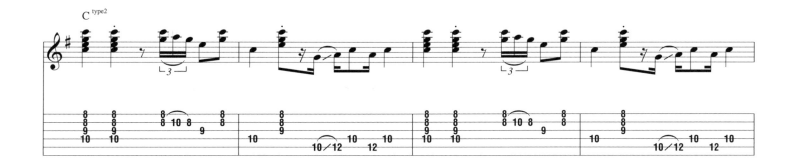

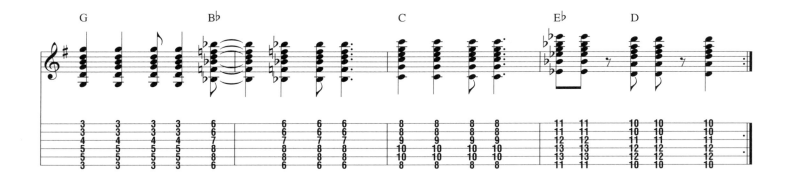

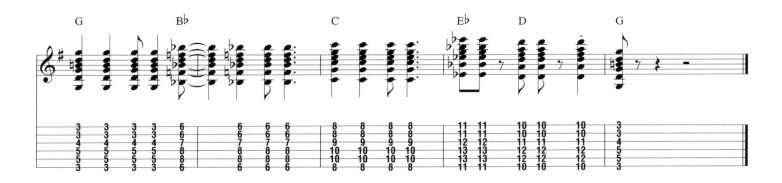

LEAD GUITAR STYLES

The lead guitar part to "Sweet Soul Song" is comprised of riffs that are constructed from major and minor 6th intervals—the outside (top and bottom) notes of the chord inversions. The 6ths follow the chords of the progression. The tune ends with a repeated, descending 6ths riff.

As you learn this tune, pay close attention to which inversions you are playing.

SWEET SOUL SONG
Lead

TRACK 10
Slow Tempo

TRACK 11
Full Tempo

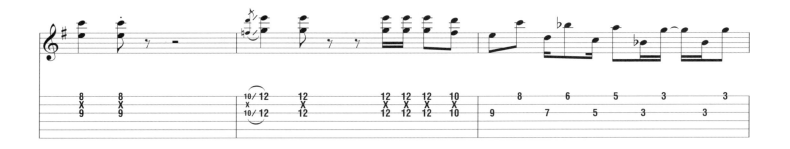

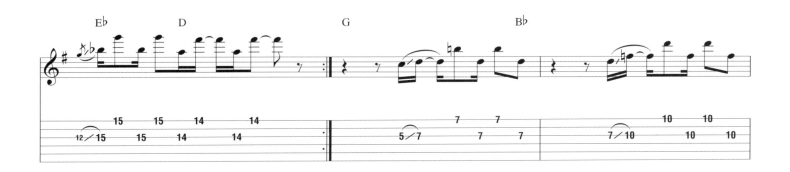

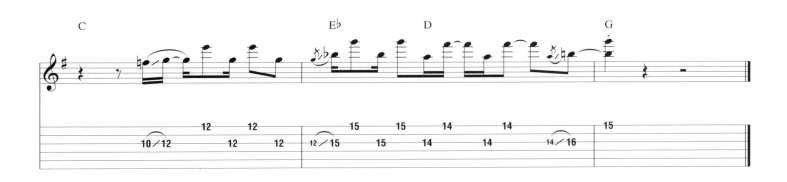

LESSON 6

Now we'll look at a syncopated, high-energy tune. "Sixties Dance Music" is an example of the early to mid '60s-style dance music. There's nothing subtle about the rhythm—it's a full-out dance beat, with lots of accents on the upbeats. The tune contains an intro and what is known as a *tag ending*, or simply a "tag," which is a Coda, or Codetta—something "tagged on" to the end of the tune.

"Sixties Dance Music" has a I–vi–IV–V chord progression, which was commonly used in R&B of the '50s and '60s. The vi chord is a "secondary chord," which is explained in the Chords section of this lesson. In addition to R&B styles, this chord movement is used in numerous popular songs and early rock 'n' roll and doo-wop music. In fact, the progression is commonly found in jazz and classical music as well.

You may notice that there is an extra bar in the repetition of the A section. The second iteration is nine bars long, as opposed to the eight bars of the first passage. The addition of an extra bar is not terribly uncommon in R&B music, and perhaps is an outgrowth of the blues. In R&B music, there is a less strict notion of form. Although structurally sound, the form is a little more free, especially in the earlier New Orleans styles. However, the freer structure can be heard in almost any R&B style.

The B section, or bridge, is nine bars long as well. Usually you would expect an eight-bar bridge, but again we have the free sense of form described above. After the bridge, the tune returns to the A section, followed by the tag. With the exception of the extra bars, this is a common song form.

THE SCALES

At this point, you should have learned all of the major pentatonic chord/scales. Now we'll combine two adjacent patterns to make larger six- and seven-fret shapes on the fingerboard. The advantage to learning them this way is that you have two chord shapes, instead of one, and a larger area on the neck with a wider range of notes. You can move and slide between the two smaller patterns.

On the next page are examples of how to combine Patterns 1 and 2 and Patterns 4 and 5. After you have worked through those examples, combine the other patterns on your own, playing through them the same way.

Two-Pattern Chord/Scale Combinations
A major pentatonic chord/scales

Pattern 2
(with D chord shape)

Patterns 1 and 2 combined

Pattern 1
(with 6th-str. root barre chord)

*from Pattern 1

continue through all keys...

D major pentatonic chord/scales

Pattern 5
(with G chord shape)

Patterns 4 and 5 combined

Pattern 4
(with 5th-str. root barre chord)

*from Pattern 4

continue through all keys...

THE CHORDS

You should know the I, IV, and V chords of all the keys—the *primary chords* of the key. In a major key, they are all of the major chords (or dominant seventh chords, which you'll learn in a later lesson). Every key also contains *secondary chords*, which are the ii, iii, and vi chords, as well as vii and ♭VII chords. We'll concern ourselves only with the ♭VII chord since, of the two chords, it's the only one that is used much in R&B tunes—even then, it's not used very often.

Lower case Roman numerals indicate a minor chord (i.e., I = major chord, i = minor chord). Also, for a very different effect, any of the secondary chords may be made major.

Here is a table of the secondary chords in every key:

Key	ii chord	iii chord	vi chord	♭VII chord
C	Dm	Em	Am	B♭
G	Am	Bm	Em	F
D	Em	F♯m	Bm	C
A	Bm	C♯m	F♯m	G
E	F♯m	G♯m	C♯m	D
B	C♯m	D♯m	G♯m	A
F♯/G♭	G♯m/A♭m	A♯m/B♭m	D♯m/E♭m	E/F♭
D♭	E♭m	Fm	B♭m	C♭
A♭	B♭m	Cm	Fm	G♭
E♭	Fm	Gm	Cm	D♭
B♭	Cm	Dm	Gm	A♭
F	Gm	Am	Dm	E♭

This concept was introduced in Lesson 18 of *Blues You Can Use* and more thoroughly explained in *Blues You Can Use: Guitar Chords*—both books in this series—and especially in *Jazzin' the Blues*, which I co-wrote with my good friend and master jazz guitarist, David Roos. If you are interested in learning more, you can refer to them.

Using the above chart, find all of the chords of the major keys. To help you get started, on the next page are some ways to put them together. There are many, many more arrangements, however.

Primary and Secondary Chords

6th-string-root chords, key of F major

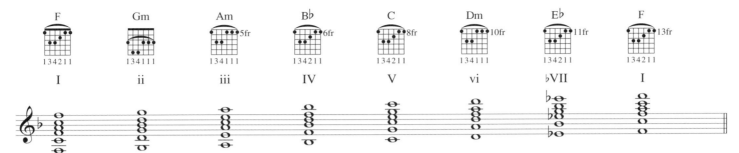

5th-string-root chords, key of B♭ major

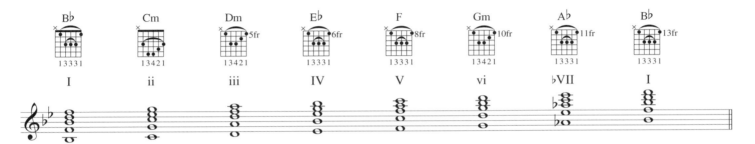

Combination 6th-, 5th-, and 4th-string-root chords, key of A major

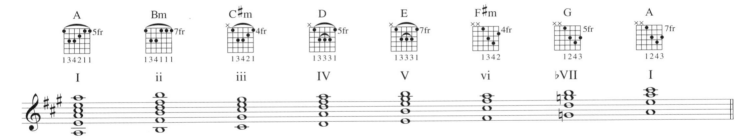

RHYTHM GUITAR STYLES

The chords that are used in "Sixties Dance Music" are of the same type as the chords that we have been using throughout this book. The progression is I–vi–IV–V, using the secondary chords that were introduced in this lesson. The song is written in the key of A major, so the chords are A (I), F♯m (vi), D (IV), and E (V).

The distinguishing element, and what gives this tune much of its character, is the *syncopated* rhythm. *Syncopation* is an accent, strum, or note that occurs in an unexpected or irregular place in the music.

The rhythm is also a shuffle (often called a *swing feel*), which is indicated above the music notation in parentheses as two eighth notes equal a quarter and eighth note under a triplet bracket. This concept is covered thoroughly in *Blues You Can Use* (see Lesson 4), but if you're unsure, listen to the CD track to get a sense of how the shuffle should sound.

A two-bar strumming pattern is used through most of the tune. It occurs in the intro and stays on the I chord (A). Once you move into the body of the tune, or verse, the chords change each time you repeat the rhythm cycle as the song moves through the I–vi–IV–V progression. In other words, the chords change every two bars.

Strum with a downstroke on the downbeats, and with an upstroke on the upbeats. That is, at the beginning of the beat—on 1, 2, 3, and 4—strum downward. On the upbeats, the "&" of the beat, strum in an upward direction. This helps you to keep track of where you are within the beat and gives you a stronger sense of the upbeats and downbeats.

Start by working slowly through "Sixties Dance Music," gradually increasing the speed. Be sure that you have full control of the strumming, even if that means taking the song at a painfully slow tempo at first.

SIXTIES DANCE MUSIC
Rhythm

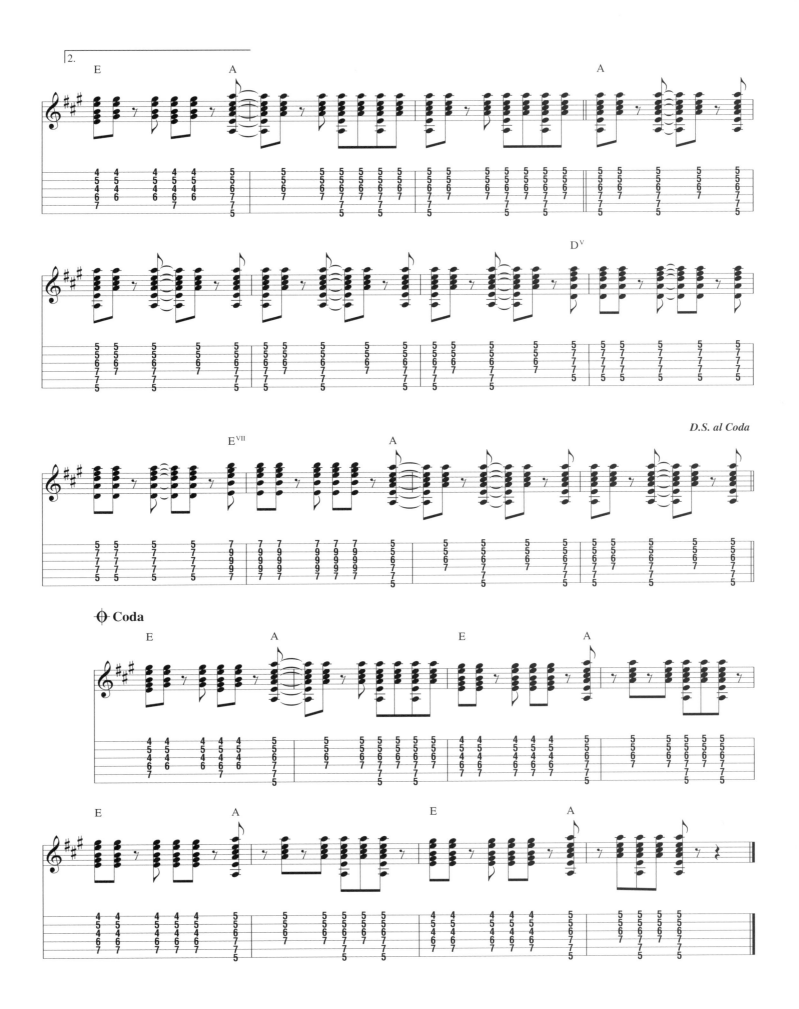

LEAD GUITAR STYLES

The lead guitar solo enters with a little pick-up riff at the very end of the intro. This riff has a triplet figure that is repeated throughout the A section and notes that are derived almost exclusively from the pentatonic scales related to the individual chords.

SIXTIES DANCE MUSIC
Lead

D.S. al Coda

Coda

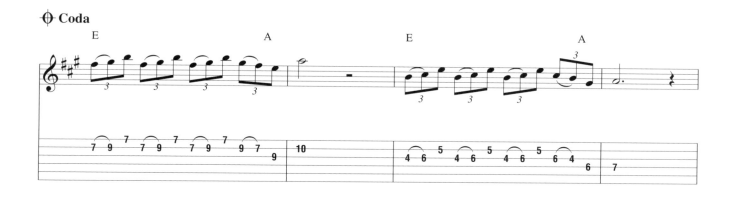

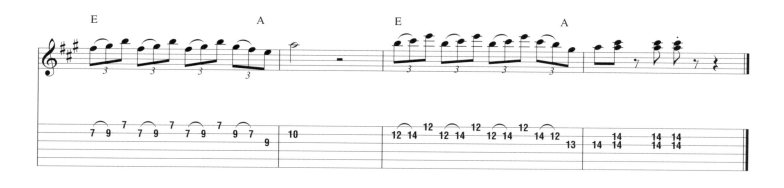

LESSON 7

"It's About Time," this lesson's study, is another I–vi–IV–V progression—this time in the key of C major. It consists of "chord chops" and short, two-note bass runs, which move from chord to chord.

The lead solo weaves through the chord progression, following the changes and making use of common notes among the scales. It is very much blues-based, though played over something other than a 12-bar blues progression.

THE SCALES

As you play through the scale patterns, keep moving between patterns and to different positions, which will help you to avoid "ruts" and playing the same old licks over and over. Every time you move, new possibilities arise. The notes are organized differently and each position contains different pitch ranges. To help you get started, here are two exercises, one in A major pentatonic and the other in D major pentatonic. The scale patterns are marked.

Playing Major Pentatonic Scales Along the Fingerboard

A major pentatonic scale

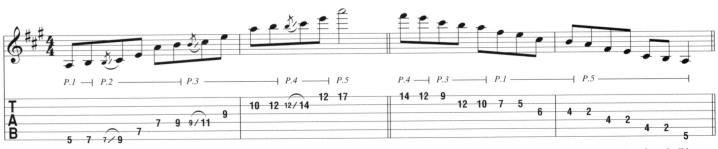

continue through all keys...

D major pentatonic scale

continue through all keys...

THE CHORDS

If you take the three-note chords that you learned in Lesson 5 and play *just* the outside notes, you'll end up with the interval of a 6th. An *interval* is the distance between two notes, or two notes played simultaneously or sequentially. The former (simultaneous) are called *harmonic intervals*, and the latter (sequential) are *melodic intervals*.

Take a look at the following example to see how that works.

6ths in Chord Shapes
on strings 3–1

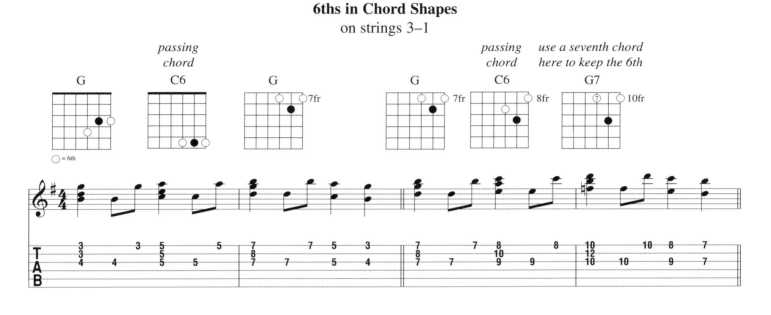

on strings 4–2

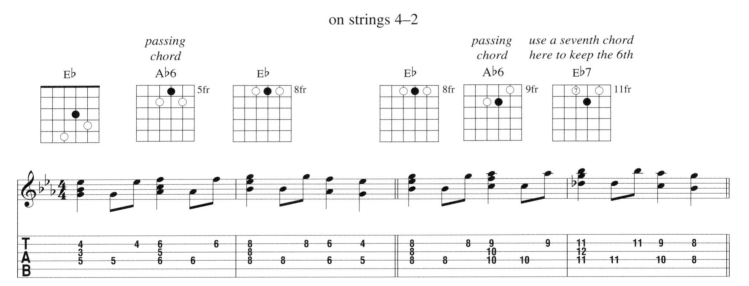

Major and minor 6th intervals are often used in R&B-style tunes. Sixth intervals were introduced in Lesson 16 of *Blues You Can Use* and further explored in Lesson 8 of *More Blues You Can Use*.

It is important to see 6ths in relation to their chord shapes. That way, you'll be able to use them for any chord, in any key. Below are two exercises to help you learn them.

6ths in Chord Shapes Exercise
on strings 3–1

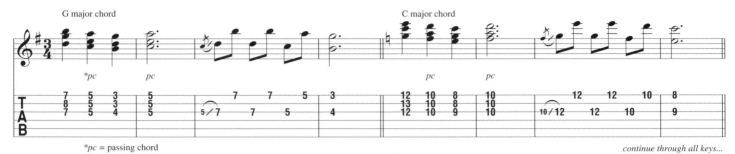

*pc = passing chord

continue through all keys...

on strings 4–2

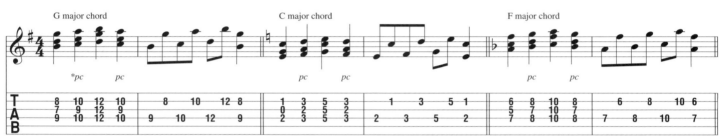

*pc = passing chord

continue through all keys...

RHYTHM GUITAR STYLES

The I–vi–IV–V progression can repeat endlessly because it moves smoothly and strongly from one chord to the next, ending on a V chord, which of course wants to move to a I chord. The V chord can signal either another repeat of the cycle, a move into another chord sequence, or the final ending chord.

The rhythm guitar part to "It's About Time" is a simple chop-type rhythm, leaving lots of space for a soloist or a singer to move around in. The chop falls on the second and fourth beats of the bar, giving the tune forward momentum. Beats 2 and 4 are the "backbeats," which define the fundamental rhythm of both rock 'n' roll and R&B, as well as the blues—it's what Chuck Berry declared you must have for "rock and roll music" in his song of the same title.

Note that, while the score is notated in 12/8 time, that meter is just for convenience. What it really represents is 4/4 time with a triplet feel or subdivision of the beat, which you learned in Lesson 2.

As you play "It's About Time," make sure to give a good accent to the chops, without becoming overbearing.

IT'S ABOUT TIME

Rhythm

TRACK 14
Slow Tempo

TRACK 15
Full Tempo

LEAD GUITAR STYLES

This lead guitar part is melodic and demonstrates how you can follow the chord changes as you solo in an R&B setting. Usually, solos are taken by keyboard instruments, or most often, a saxophone. You do hear guitar solos though.

The I–vi–IV–V progression offers some interesting possibilities in your solos. To begin with, the notes of a C major pentatonic scale, which you could use over the I chord, are the same as those of the A minor pentatonic scale, which goes with the vi (Am) chord. You can play a lick in C major and continue with it over the A minor chord, using the same set of notes. You can even repeat a riff, once over the C major chord, and then over the A minor chord. Although the notes are exactly the same, the riff sounds very different over each chord.

For the IV and V chords, their corresponding major pentatonic scales are used. You simply could use the C major/A minor pentatonic scale throughout the solo and it would work fine, but you wouldn't get the rich, varied sound that you do when you change scales with the chords. This approach is essentially how jazz players form their solos.

IT'S ABOUT TIME

Lead

TRACK 14
Slow Tempo

TRACK 15
Full Tempo

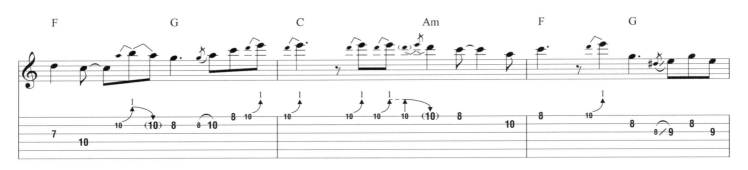

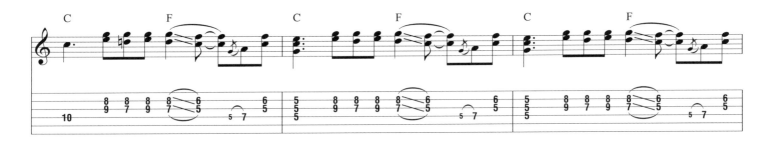

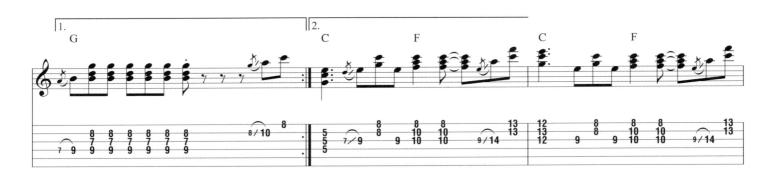

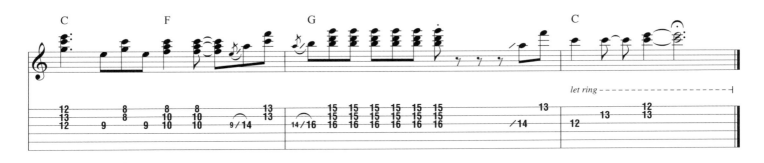

This lesson's study, "Crescent City Rhythm," is written in early '60s New Orleans style. It has a bounce to it, with syncopated chord strums.

After a four-bar intro, "Crescent City Rhythm" contains two sections: an "A" section, followed by a bridge, or "B" section. The A section is more extensive and repeated before you go to the bridge. After the bridge, the A section is played a third time. "Crescent City Rhythm" is a common song form that is used in popular music, including R&B styles. The structure is referred to as "AABA" song form because you play the A section twice, followed by one repetition of the B section and a return to the A section. In this tune, the Coda (ending) is a reprise of the intro—not an uncommon practice.

THE SCALES

In the same way that we built major pentatonic chord/scales, minor pentatonic chord/scales can be built from minor pentatonic scales and chords. In this case, the scales have *minor* chords embedded in them. Here's what they look like in the key of G minor:

Minor Pentatonic Chord/Scales Along the Fingerboard

ℝ = root

Pattern 1   Pattern 2   Pattern 3   Pattern 4   Pattern 5

You can work through the minor pentatonic chord/scales in the same way that you did the major pentatonic chord/scales, as illustrated in the following exercise. After you practice Pattern 1, work out exercises for the remaining four patterns.

Minor Pentatonic Chord/Scale Study
Pattern 1

Key of G Minor:
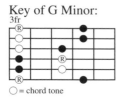
○ = chord tone

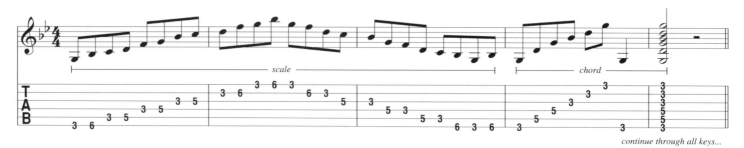

continue through all keys...

THE CHORDS

We've seen major and minor triads and sixth chords so far. Now we're going to look at another commonly used chord type—the add9. Its construction is very simple; you just add a 9th to a major or minor triad. If you have played much blues—and you really should have—you undoubtedly have played ninth chords. The 9th from that chord is the same note that we use in an add9 chord. The important difference between the two is that the add9 chord does not contain a 7th, which makes the chord sound very different—pretty and chiming. Usually, the 9th is added as the top voice (note) of the chord. You can add a 9th to a major or a minor chord. Here are a few voicings:

Add9 Chord Voicings

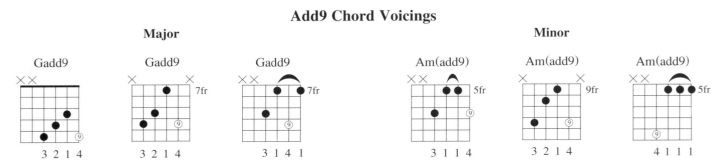

Now here's an exercise to show you how to use them. All of the voicings are in root position.

Major and Minor Add9 Chords

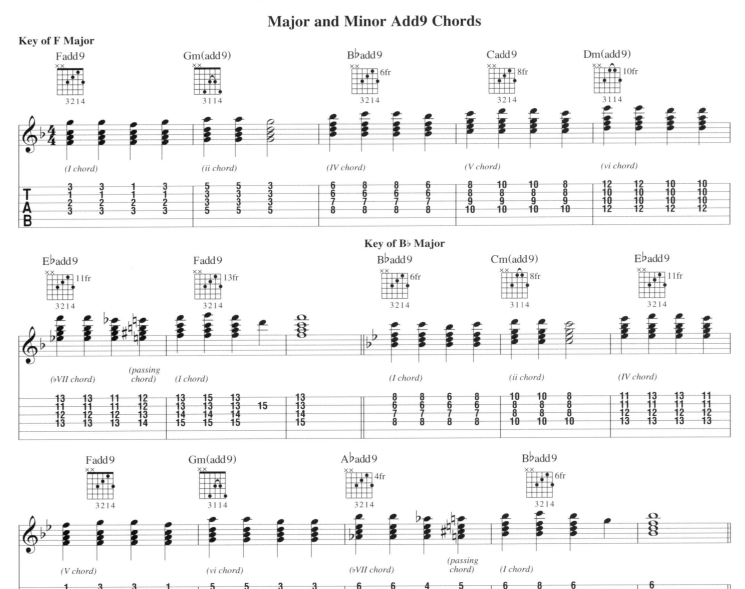

continue through all keys...

RHYTHM GUITAR STYLES

We use major barre chords in "Crescent City Rhythm," as we did in the last lesson. The sixth-string-root chords are best played with your thumb fretting the bass (lowest) note. The reason for this is that you need the rest of your fingers unencumbered to play the chordal articulations in the tune. This is an active rhythm.

Again, we use the major pentatonic scale over or just above the chord shape—this time, to add some single notes to the rhythm part. For the sixth-string chords, Pattern 1 is used. The fifth-string chords are played with Pattern 5, with the addition of the low root, which is just down the neck from the pattern.

In measure 17, take note of the bass run into the bridge, which is repeated in measure 25, where the chord progression of the bridge is repeated. Simply let go of the chord and play the run, which is constructed of octaves—a topic that will be covered in Lesson 10. You'll find that using your thumb for the notes on the sixth string enables you to be in position to finger the B♭ chord at the end of the run.

CRESCENT CITY RHYTHM
Rhythm

LEAD GUITAR STYLES

In the lead guitar part to "Crescent City Rhythm," the major pentatonic scales are used the same way as the last study—they follow the chord changes and are connected to the chord shapes themselves. The lead part provides some funky rhythmic fills and punctuation.

After the bridge, the song returns to the A section, where the first 12 bars are repeated. After that, you take it out with the tag ending (Coda).

CRESCENT CITY RHYTHM
Lead

TRACK 16
Slow Tempo

TRACK 17
Full Tempo

Now let's take a look at a little funky, rhythm-style soul. "Funky Soul" is a 20-bar form with a four-bar intro and a four-bar tag ending. There's a strong syncopated feel to this one, due to the fact that many of the chords are strummed on upbeats. Also contributing to the feel is the technique of approaching the chords via half steps (one fret). "Funky Soul" should be played with energy and excitement. The idea of a tune like this is to provide a very danceable beat, and this one does it.

THE SCALES

You can put the adjacent minor pentatonic chord/scales together in units, just like we did with the major pentatonic chord/scales in Lesson 6. That approach works the same way and has the same advantages (more note choices and two embedded chords). Here are two examples. One example is a combination of Patterns 1 and 2, and the other combines Patterns 3 and 4. Once you've learned them, combine the other adjacent patterns.

Two-Pattern Minor Chord/Scale Combinations
B minor pentatonic chord/scales
(6th-string root)

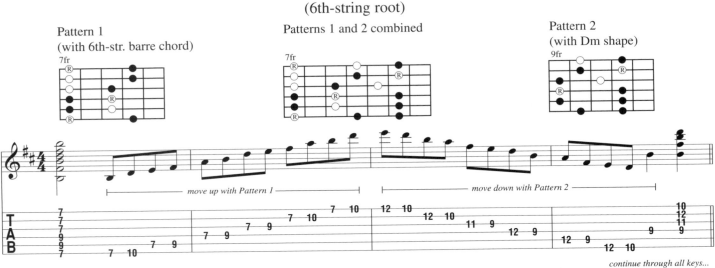

continue through all keys...

E minor pentatonic chord/scales
(5th-string root)

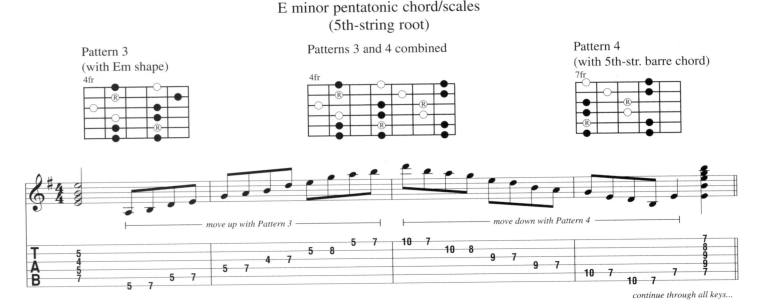

continue through all keys...

THE CHORDS

You've now learned the basic triads, sixth chords, and major and minor add9 chords. Now we're going to look at how all of them work together in four-note chord shapes. You also will be introduced to the sus4 chord. All of the chords are built on the top strings.

The sus4 ("suspended" 4) is found above the 3rd of the chord. In a major chord, it is located one half step (one fret) above the 3rd. Because the 3rd is flatted (lowered) one fret in a minor chord, the sus4 is located one whole step (two frets) above the 3rd. The example below contains all of the major chords.

Major Triads with Added Chord Tones

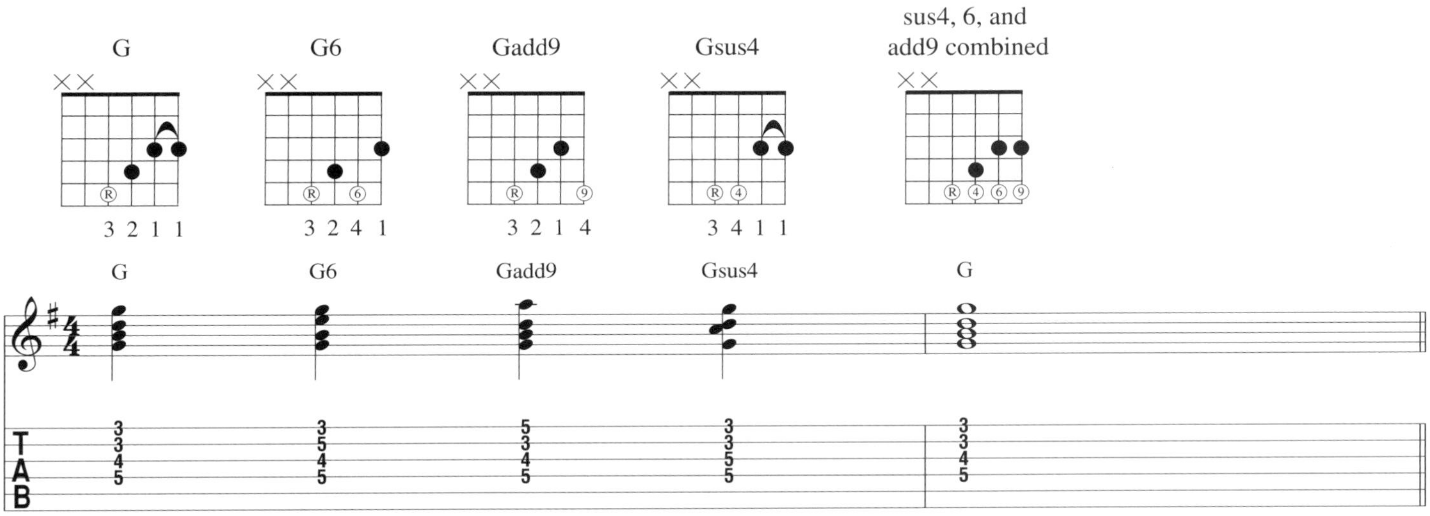

The same notes are added to minor chords, with exception of the sixth. In R&B styles, minor sixth chords are not used much at all because of their dissonance. Instead, a 7th is used. Adding a 7th to a minor triad doesn't change its function in the key. Theoretically, whenever a minor chord is required, you can use a minor seventh chord, though it will sound quite different and may not sound "right."

The diagram below illustrates how the sus4, 7th, and 9th chord tones are added to a minor triad.

Minor Triads with Added Chord Tones

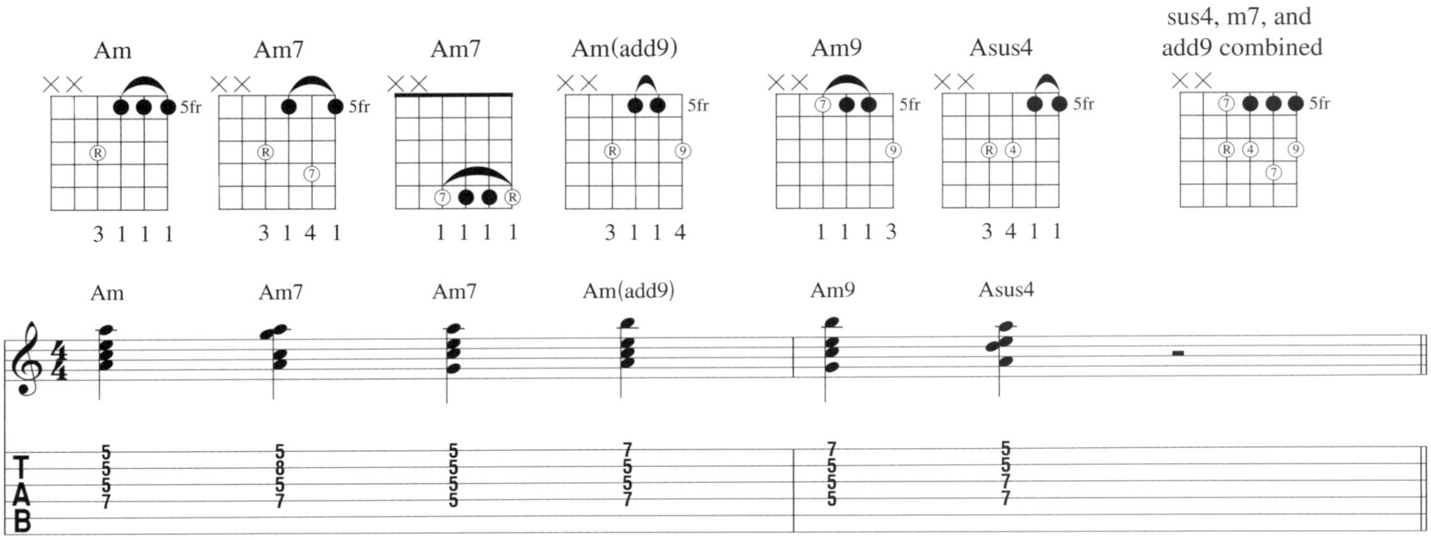

You may have noticed that the added tones are mostly the notes of the major pentatonic or minor pentatonic scales. The difference is that the notes are thought of in terms of their relationship to the chords, and in most cases, are added after the chord is fretted. Below is an exercise that will teach you how to use these added notes.

Major and Minor Added Chord Tone Exercise

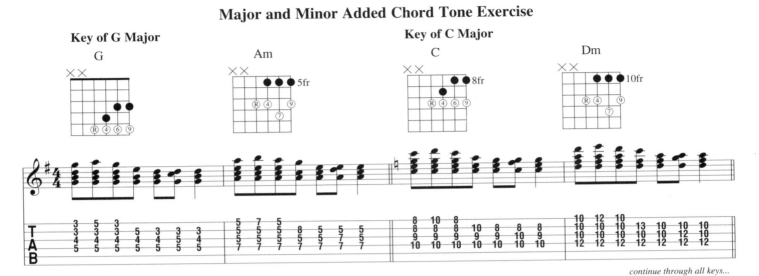

continue through all keys...

RHYTHM GUITAR STYLES

This rhythm guitar part uses big block seventh chords on the I (tonic) chord, combined with 9ths for the IV and V chords, which gives the song a big, full, driving sound, creating the dance beat described earlier. The 20-bar form is neither terribly common nor all that unusual. The intro simply cycles through the inversions of the C7 (I) chord in order, starting on the root-position chord. The Coda is identical to the intro.

As you play through the tune, remember to keep a light touch in your left (fret) hand. Consequently, you'll be able to move much more quickly and adroitly from chord to chord. You'll also achieve a better tone.

FUNKY SOUL
Rhythm

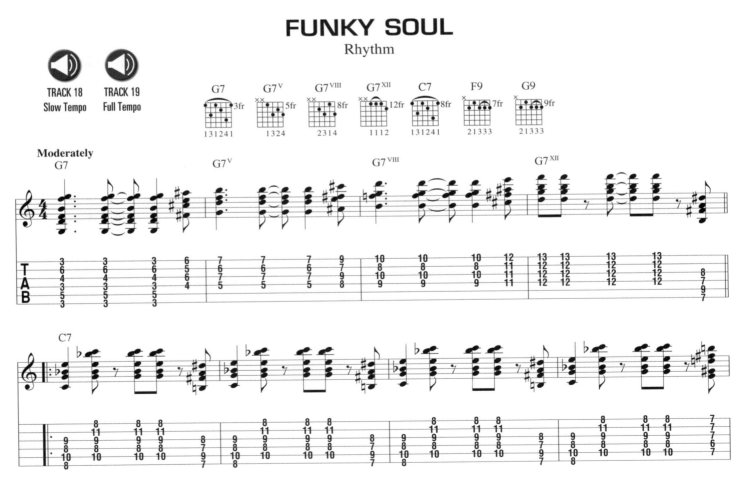

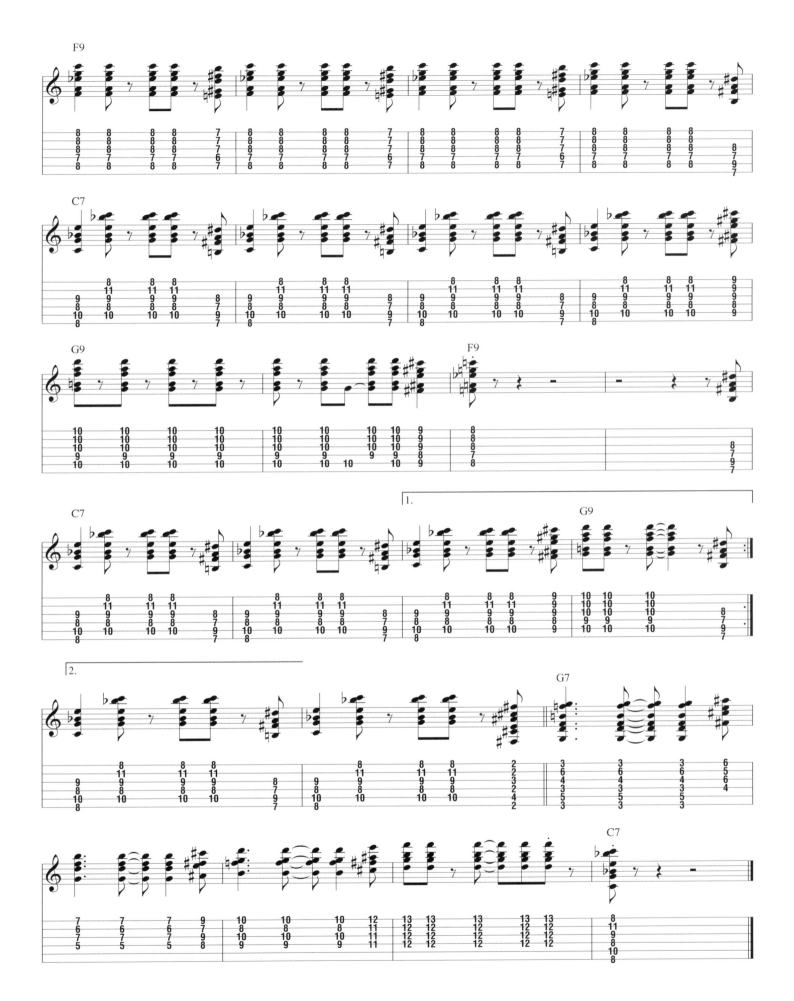

55

LEAD GUITAR STYLES

The lead guitar part to "Funky Soul" is just a funky, soul-style, minor pentatonic solo full of blues-based riffs. It has a sixteenth-note feel, a crisp rhythm, and the licks repeat in different octave registers. This lead part is more like a blues solo, in that it stays in the same key, which is "forced" over the chord progression. The exceptions are the 6ths licks, which follow the chord changes.

In this tune, crisp, sharp rhythm is key.

FUNKY SOUL
Lead

TRACK 18
Slow Tempo

TRACK 19
Full Tempo

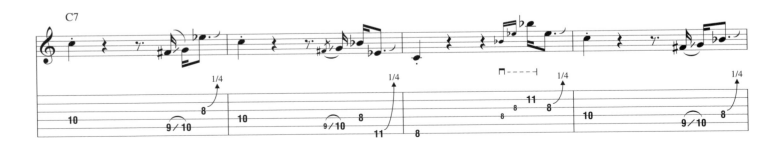

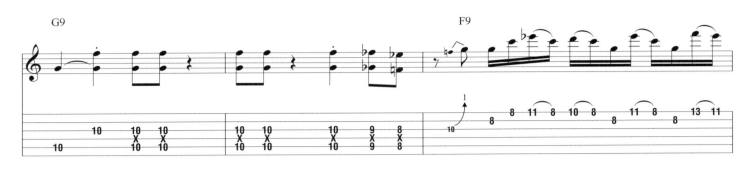

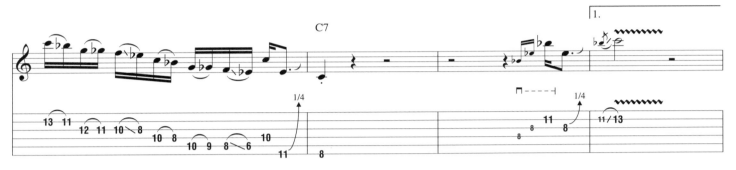

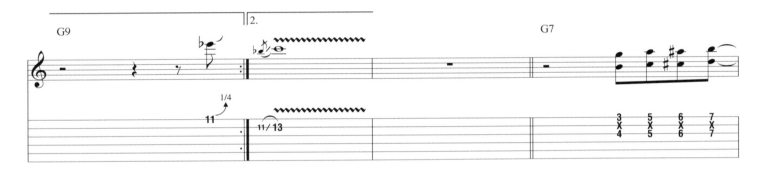

Essentially a dance tune, "Groovin' Funk," this lesson's study, has a funky rhythm reminiscent of some of those heard in New Orleans soul. You are probably getting the idea that an awful lot of the R&B styles had their birth in the Crescent City, a musical and overall cultural treasure chest, with jazz, blues, and R&B having many of their deepest roots there.

After the four-bar intro, the tune takes an AABA form, followed by a six-bar tag ending.

THE SCALES

When playing melodic single-note lines, you can double them by playing the same note an octave higher or lower. A note's octave is found 12 half steps (frets) above or below it and has the same letter name. For example, the open sixth string is an E note. The note at the 12th fret of string 6 is also an E, one octave higher. A more practical location is two strings and two frets up. If the second string is involved, either by playing on it, using strings 4 and 2, or across it, using strings 3 and 1, the octave is located three frets up. They look like this:

Octaves on the Fingerboard

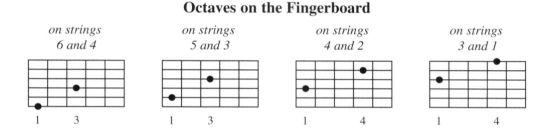

| on strings 6 and 4 | on strings 5 and 3 | on strings 4 and 2 | on strings 3 and 1 |

You can use scales to practice the octave shapes. Below are octave exercises, using major and minor pentatonic chord/scales. Once you've learned them, you can create your own.

Follow the fingerings, which are located between the notation and tab staves. If you wish, you may use your own, but keep them consistent like those in the exercises. Also, make sure that you use a light touch when fretting the octaves, which will enable you to play them more smoothly.

Octave Exercise
C major pentatonic scale

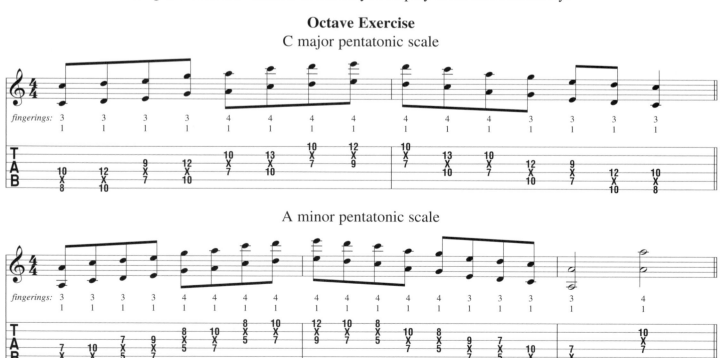

A minor pentatonic scale

THE CHORDS

You saw how to add the sus4, 6th, and 9th chord tones to root-position triads to create a more active and melodic rhythm part. Now we'll look at adding them to chord inversions. Although the chord shapes are different, the approach is the same.

Major and Minor Triad Inversions with Added Chord Tones

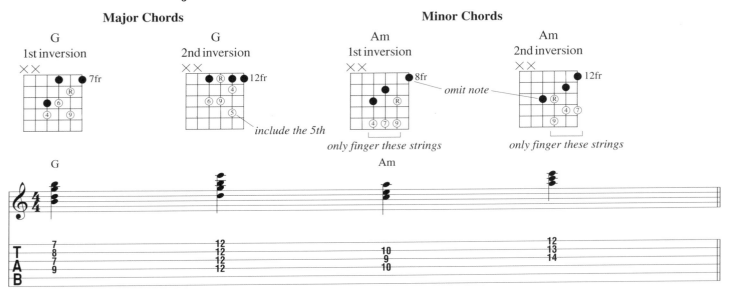

Now here's an exercise combining root-position and first-inversion major and minor chords with the added tones. Create and experiment with your own chord movements.

Major and Minor Chords with Added Tones

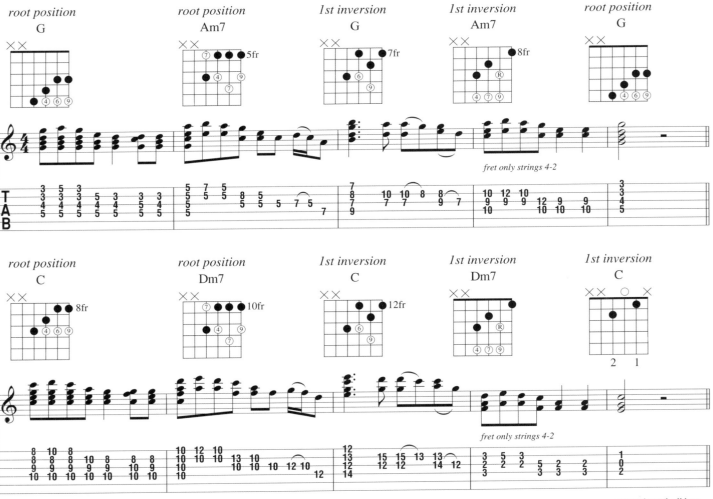

continue through all keys...

RHYTHM GUITAR STYLES

The rhythm guitar part to "Groovin' Funk" is comprised of block seventh chords, which lend a clean, spare sound, but with a bluesy touch. The block seventh chords are mostly reached via an "approach chord," which also is a seventh type. An *approach chord* is a chord that leads into another "target" chord, usually a half step away. Approach chords are almost always the same type of voicing as the target chord. The approach chord is not part of the progression and doesn't qualify as a chord change; it simply is a chordal embellishment.

The strums in "Groovin' Funk" are syncopated, giving the rhythm a forward momentum and drive. That's what makes it danceable.

Notice how parts of the larger chords in the score are strummed—some are on the upper strings and some on the lower. This approach gives you what amounts to different chord voicings when, in fact, you form a single shape on the fingerboard. Be sure to play a chop on the syncopated strums.

GROOVIN' FUNK
Rhythm

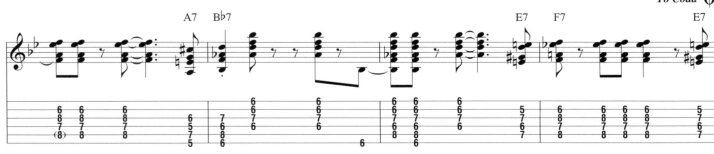

LEAD GUITAR STYLES

The lead guitar part to "Groovin' Funk" is composed of short, supporting lines. They're not really melodies; instead, they're little licks that act as fills and help create a bigger sound, or "wall." The licks are played with octaves, where the notes of the lines are doubled an octave apart, lending an even bigger sound to the lead. Play the octaves with a very light touch and with staccato technique, cutting them short and disconnecting them from each other. Octaves require some practice, so be patient.

GROOVIN' FUNK
Lead

TRACK 20
Slow Tempo

TRACK 21
Full Tempo

The tune for this lesson, "Minor Soul Chop," is in a minor key and contains a V chord that is both minor (vm7) and dominant (V7). Compared to the minor seventh chord, the dominant seventh chord offers a much stronger movement to the i chord.

The tune begins with a four-bar intro that consists of a i–vm7 chord vamp. The body of the tune is an eight-bar form, which is repeated, followed by a four-bar Codetta (a short Coda), also consisting of the i–vm7 vamp.

Because of the repeated i–vm7 chord phrases and the use of rests between chord chops, "Minor Soul Chop" has a sparse, open, and, due to its minor tonality, a rather haunting sound (deep reverb helps, too). Try to cultivate that sound while you play the song.

This style was heard throughout the '60s, from artists such as New Orleans singers Irma Thomas and Sam Cooke to the "Godfather of Soul," James Brown.

THE SCALES

Now we'll look at some ways to practice the major pentatonic chord/scales. Once you have learned the form of a chord/scale by playing it up and down the pattern, start to create little riffs or melodic figures/fragments, playing them in every key. This way, you begin to use the chord/scales musically, instead of mechanically running up and down the shape. Following are three exercises that illustrate this idea.

Major Chord/Scale Practice Routines

Pattern 1
Major Pentatonic Scale:

continue through all keys...

Pattern 5   ------ to ------   Pattern 1
Major Pentatonic Scale: Major Pentatonic Scale:

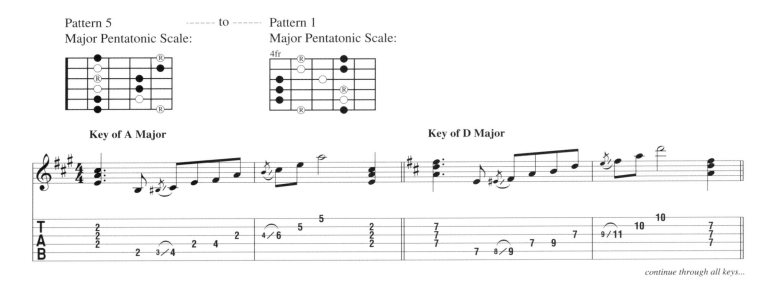

continue through all keys...

Pattern 3
Major Pentatonic Scale:

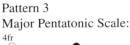
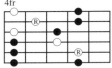

continue through all keys...

THE CHORDS

Chord substitutions are instances when a chord is played in place of the original chord. Substitutions add interest to the progression, and various theoretical reasons explain how and why they work. Here we'll look at the I–IV–I substitution.

The I–IV–I substitution actually involves using a IV chord as a substitute for the I chord. That is, for a very brief moment, you can substitute the IV chord for the I chord before returning to the I chord. The IV chord isn't considered a "chord change" in the truest sense (you are still considered to be on the I chord); instead, it is simply intended to add interest to the chord progression.

Even though this chordal approach is referred to as a "IV chord substitution," the substituted chord doesn't have to be the IV chord of the key, subbing for the I chord. Instead, the IV chord substitution moves to the *IV chord of the chord you are on*. For example, if you are in the key of A major, the V chord is an E chord. You can substitute that E chord with its own IV chord, A, as though you were in the key of E major for that moment. We call that maneuver *IV of V*.

You can use the IV relative to any chord, even minor (e.g., IV of IV, IV of vi, IV of ii). This substitution is not as complicated as it may sound. Here's what it looks like in the key of A major:

Chord of the Key	IV in "Momentary Key"	Substitution
I = A	IV in the key of A major = D	IV of I = D
IV = D	IV in the key of D major = G	IV of IV = G
V = E	IV in the key of E major = A	IV of V = A
ii = Bm	iv in the key of B minor = Em	iv of ii = Em
vi = F♯m	iv in the key of F♯ minor = Bm	iv of vi = Bm

Let that soak in for a minute. Then look at the following examples, which demonstrate some of the ways that the substitutions lay on the fretboard. Many possibilities exist, so you should start to look for others on your own. You also can find them on pages 75–76 of *Blues You Can Use: Guitar Chords*.

I–IV–I Substitution
(key of A major)

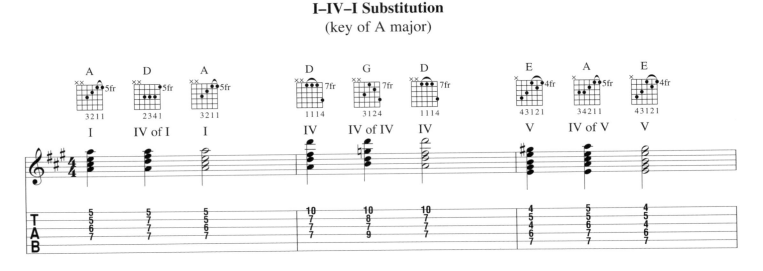

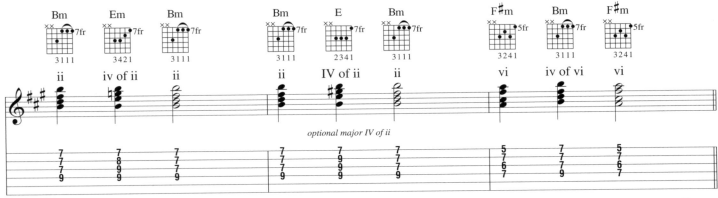

transpose to all keys...

RHYTHM GUITAR STYLES

The chord chops in the rhythm guitar part to "Minor Soul Chop" should be clean and accented, but don't hit them so hard that you get a harsh, buzzing sound. Let the chopped chords ring briefly before cutting them off. That way, you'll hear the sound of the harmony. Listen to the audio recording for an example.

MINOR SOUL CHOP
Rhythm

TRACK 22
Slow Tempo

TRACK 23
Full Tempo

LEAD GUITAR STYLES

The lead guitar part to "Minor Soul Chop" contains "sweetening notes." They really don't create a melody that goes anywhere; instead, they simply "sweeten up" the tune, helping to support the melody as sung or played on another instrument. Here, the sweetening notes are fairly extensive, but when used in a setting with a singer, for example, you have to be careful so as not to overpower the vocals. Whenever you find a pause (rest) in the melody, you can fill it with sweetening notes. You also can play over the vocals, as long as you stay in the background and out of the way. Sweetening notes are not the main feature—that role is for the singer or soloist. The band is there to support the soloist. Sweetening notes are simply "embellishing notes," which you have been using throughout this book.

The sweetening notes in the lead to "Minor Soul Chop" are from minor chord/scales.

MINOR SOUL CHOP

Lead

TRACK 22
Slow Tempo

TRACK 23
Full Tempo

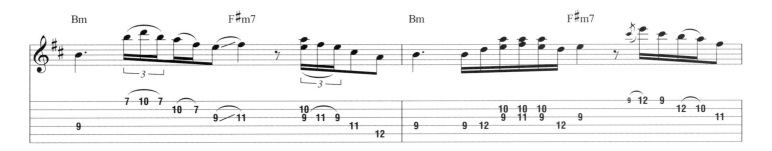

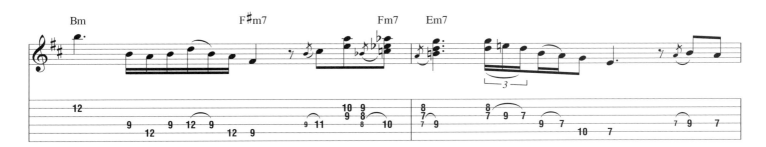

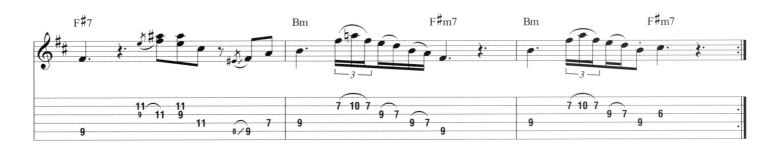

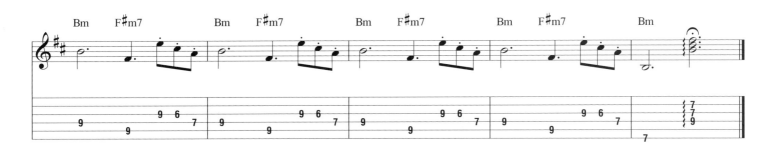

LESSON 12

The study for this lesson, "Atlantic Coast Soul," is like something that might have come out of Memphis's Stax studios. It's a slow tune in 6/8 time—like two bars of 3/4 time strung together. You count:

1 – 2 – 3 **4** – 5 – 6

Be sure to accent beats 1 and 4. This time signature, 6/8, makes it easy to use a triplet strumming pattern.

The tune has an AABA song form with a Coda.

The lead part continues our exploration of major and minor 6ths. You can be very expressive with these intervals, as you'll see later in this lesson. And blues licks are interspersed throughout the B section.

THE SCALES

Here we will look at a few ways that you can practice the minor pentatonic chord/scales, just like you did with the major ones in the last lesson. These exercises are simply intended to help you get started with making up your own. Once you begin to create your signature licks, you will be well on your way to developing your own style.

Minor Chord/Scale Practice Routines

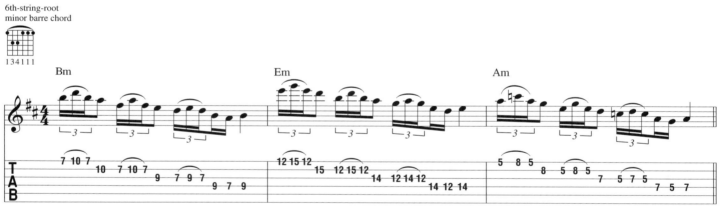

continue through all keys...

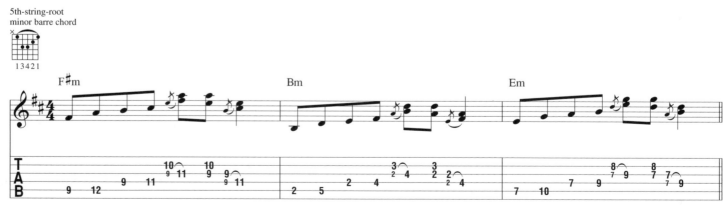

continue through all keys...

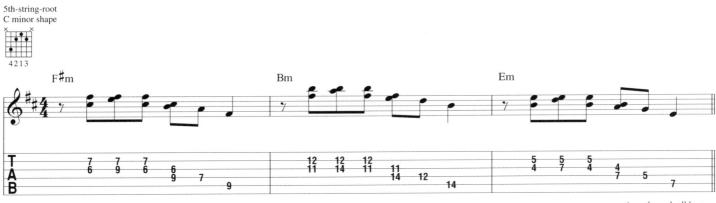

5th-string-root
C minor shape
4 2 1 3

continue through all keys...

THE CHORDS

If you come from a blues background, you should be familiar with several seventh chord voicings—at least the dominant seventh and minor seventh types. Seventh chords are used in R&B styles as well.

A seventh chord is simply a major or minor triad with the 7th chord tone tacked on. In this lesson, we will only use the ♭7th chord tone. Although later R&B styles used major seventh chords, primarily in the '70s, the styles covered in this book really didn't use them much.

If you add the ♭7th to a major triad, you get a *dominant seventh* chord. Adding the ♭7th to a minor triad results in a *minor seventh* chord. Here we'll look at four-note voicings, located on the top strings. As you look through the following diagrams, notice that the only difference between the dominant seventh and minor seventh chords is the 3rd, which is located one fret lower in the minor chords.

Seventh Chords

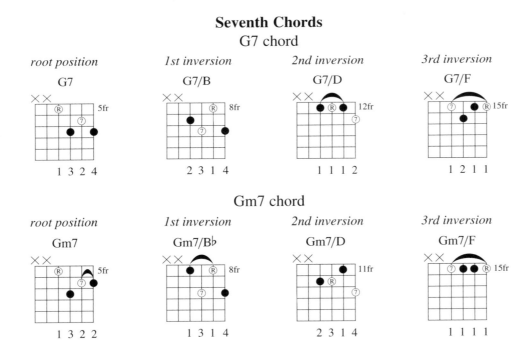

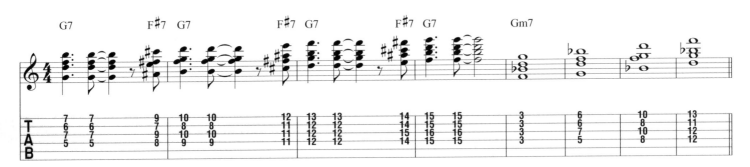

RHYTHM GUITAR STYLES

The rhythm guitar part to "Atlantic Coast Soul" consists of triplet strums of block chords. As you
learned in the previous lesson, the six-string "blocks" occasionally are strummed in smaller segments,
which results in multiple voicings of the same chord type.

ATLANTIC COAST SOUL
Rhythm

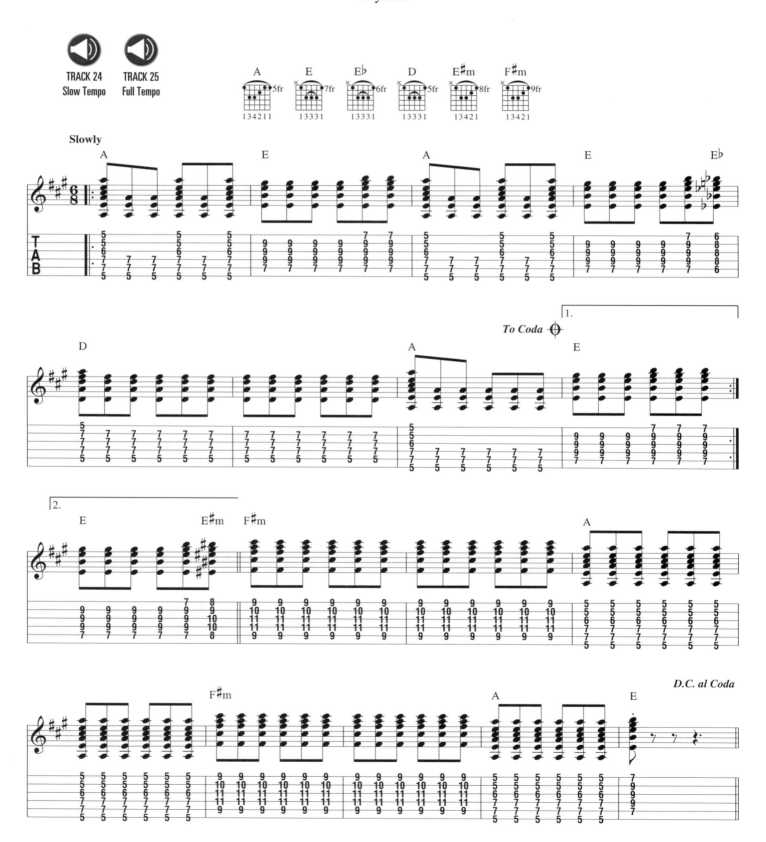

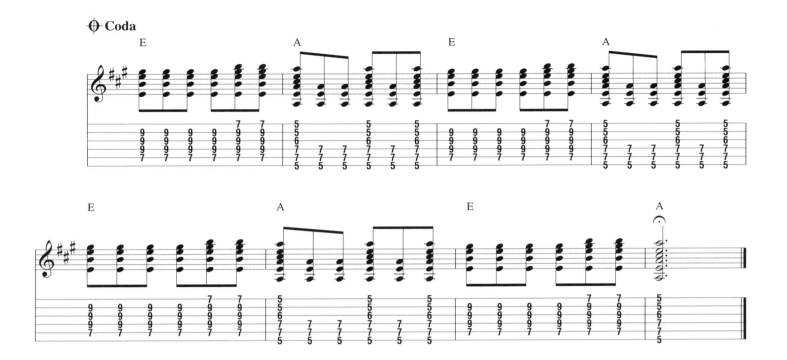

LEAD GUITAR STYLES

The lead guitar part to "Atlantic Coast Soul" is part of the accompaniment; it would be used to embellish the solo or vocals. For the most part, major and minor 6th intervals are employed to dance around the chords of the progression and to fill the spaces in the melody. The 6ths are derived from the chord shapes themselves. You already have practiced them in various ways, so they should be fairly familiar to you by now.

In measures 10 and 14, notice how blues licks are inserted for effect, using the F♯ minor pentatonic scale. Following the blues licks, the lead returns to the 6ths and a repetition of the 12-bar form, concluding with a tag ending.

ATLANTIC COAST SOUL

Lead

TRACK 24
Slow Tempo

TRACK 25
Full Tempo

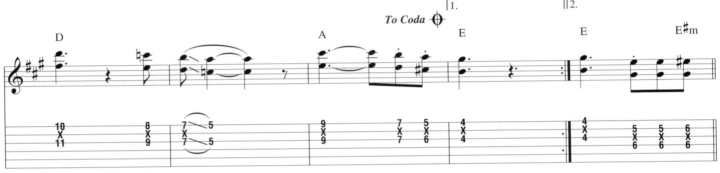

Coda

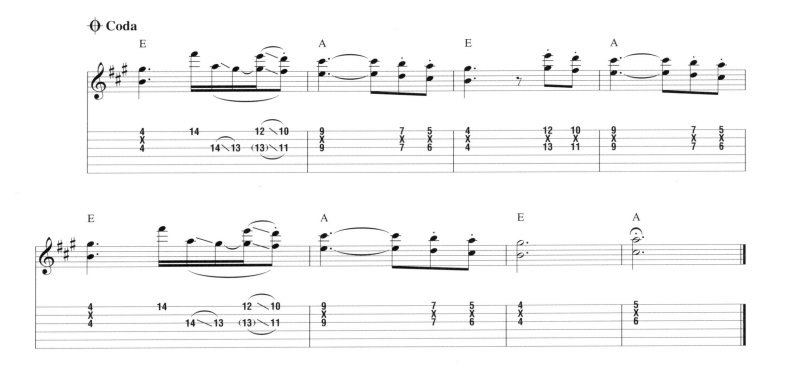

Now we're going to go back to a New Orleans R&B style. "Two-Chord Stroll," the study for this lesson, is a slow tune with a distinctive triplet rhythm. Although the tune is written in 4/4 time, each beat is divided into three sub-beats (eighth-note triplets). To make things even more complex and interesting, some of those eighth-note triplets are divided into sixteenth notes! The rhythm really is not that difficult, though, as you'll see as soon as you hear the rhythm part.

"Two-Chord Stroll" is a simple AABA song form.

THE SCALES

You may have heard of *relative minor* or *relative major* keys. Those terms refer to the relationship between a major and a minor key, which are a minor 3rd apart (three frets). The minor key is below the major. The two keys are related because they share exactly the same notes. Look at a C major pentatonic scale and its relative minor key, A minor pentatonic.

C major pentatonic: C – D – E – G – A – C

A minor pentatonic: A – C – D – E – G – A

You can see that both scales contain the same notes, only the root notes are different (see *Blues You Can Use*, pages 50–51).

Because of this relationship, you can get some interesting results by playing the same lick over the tonic chords of each key (the I of the major and the i chord of the minor), which can be thought of as a I–vi (C–Am) progression. Remember, though, that we are really thinking in terms of the chords and following their corresponding chord/scales.

Below are some examples to help you get started on creating your own major/relative minor ideas.

Licks in Major and Relative Minor Keys

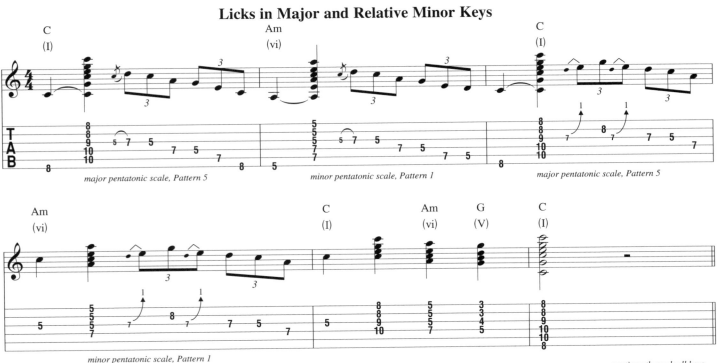

continue through all keys...

THE CHORDS

You learned all of the chords of the keys (primary and secondary) in Lesson 6. Now we'll look at using seventh chords in place of some of those chords.

You can use a seventh chord for every chord of a key, but in most R&B styles, major seventh chords are not typically used for the I and IV chords. For that reason, we'll leave them as plain major triads. Similarly, a dominant seventh chord could be substituted for the ♭VII, but like the I and IV chords, we'll stick with a major triad.

Below are the seventh chords of the keys of F, B♭, and A major. After you have learned these voicings, transpose them to the other nine keys, staying within the first 12 or 13 frets.

Seventh Chords of a Major Key
(I–iim7–iiim7–IV–V7–vim7–♭VII–♮VII–I)

6th-String Root - Key of F Major:

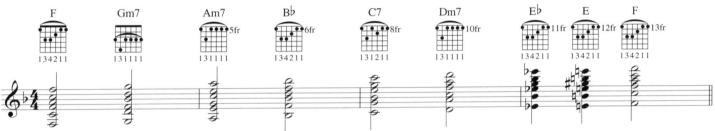

5th-String Root - Key of B♭ Major:

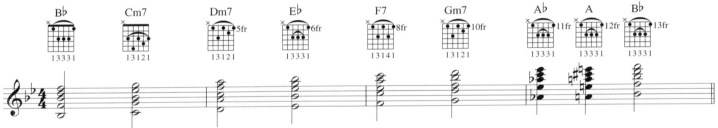

Combination 6th-, 5th-, and 4th-String Root - Key of A Major:

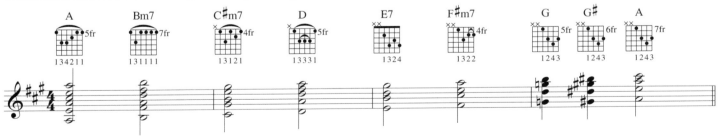

RHYTHM GUITAR STYLES

As you play the rhythm guitar part, carefully follow the strum-direction instructions, which will help you get the proper rhythmic feel. The notation is written in rhythm slashes, which should prove easier to read for this particular example. Pay close attention to the *staccato marks* (the dots located below the rhythm slashes). Those strums should be cut short, or chopped. Although this is written out in 4/4 time, you could also think of it in 6/8 or 12/8 time.

The chords in the tune are four-note, fourth-string-root chords. Due to their smaller size, four-note chords are more easily fingered and usually free up a finger to add notes, like the Am(add9) chord in the second measure.

The ii (Am) chord, a secondary chord that was introduced in Lesson 6, is used extensively here. The tune is in the key of G major.

TWO-CHORD STROLL
Rhythm

LEAD GUITAR STYLES

The lead guitar part to "Two-Chord Stroll" is very melodic, imitating a vocal part, and derived from pentatonic scales, chords, and arpeggios. Even the chords are intended to simulate back-up singers.

The fingerings are tricky. For that reason, I have included suggested fingerings. As always, feel free to change any of them; just be sure to be consistent.

TWO-CHORD STROLL

Lead

TRACK 26 Slow Tempo   **TRACK 27** Full Tempo

Moderately slow

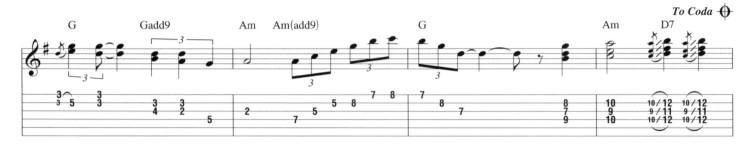

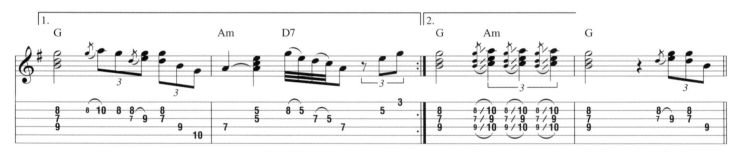

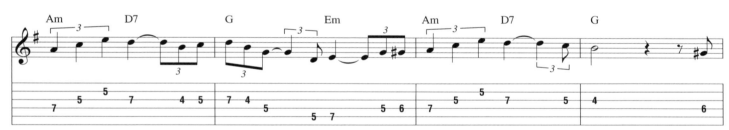

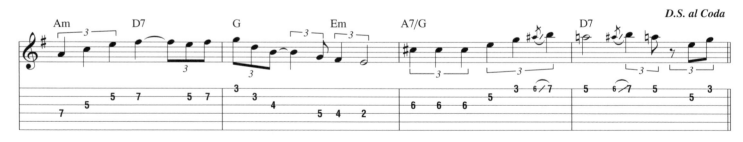

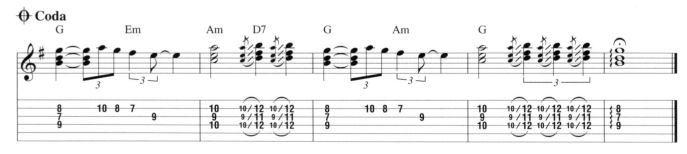

LESSON 14

In this lesson, we will change the study's time signature. Instead of 4/4 or 12/8, "Motor City Stroll" is written in 3/4 time, which means that each bar contains three beats, with the quarter notes still receiving one beat.

After a four-bar intro, the study follows an AABA form, concluding with an eight-bar Coda. In the Coda, an unorthodox IV→VI–I progression is used.

THE SCALES

Continuing the chordal approach to single-note lines, the following exercise illustrates how you might play a chord followed by a melodic line. It's very simple. You should attempt to create your own little ditties, like the ones below, which will help you develop the skills to incorporate chords into your lead parts.

Licks with Chords
Through a I–ii–IV–V

Key of A Major

Key of C Major

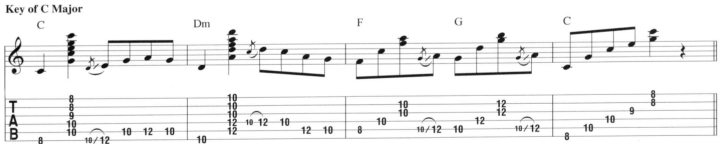

continue through keys of A♭, B, G, B♭, and G♭ major

THE CHORDS

In Lesson 7, you learned how to use 6th intervals related to triad shapes on the fingerboard. Now you'll learn how to use 6ths with dominant seventh chord shapes. The two approaches are pretty much the same, except that the sevenths are four-note chords, so you must know where the 6ths are located.

Some of the 6ths are the same as those found in the triad exercises; others contain the 7th of the chord. Below is an exercise to get you started.

6ths with Seventh Chords

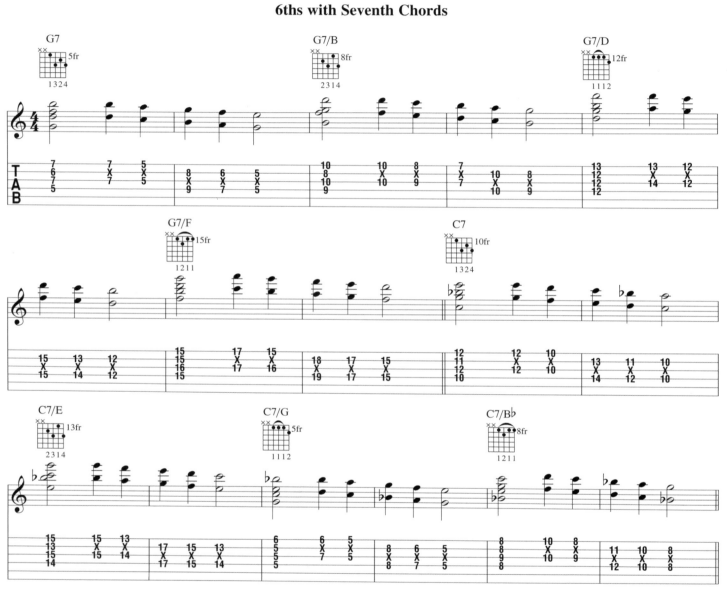

continue through all keys...

The *slash chord* symbols in the above exercise may be new to you. Slash chords are very simple. The letter and numeral to the left of the slash ("/") give the chord its name (e.g., G7 or Am9). The letter to the right of the slash is the note in the bass (bottom note) of the chord. Like the following:

NAME OF CHORD / BASS NOTE

So, if you see "G7/B," it means the chord is a G7 with a B in the bass. Slash chords enable the composer or arranger to communicate to the performer what note is to be played in the bass.

RHYTHM GUITAR STYLES

"Motor City Stroll" is an extensive study of the I–IV–I substitution that was introduced in Lesson 11, using four-note chords built on the top strings.

Remember, think in terms of the individual chords—not the key—when you use the I–IV–I substitution.

MOTOR CITY STROLL

Rhythm

TRACK 28
Slow Tempo

TRACK 29
Full Tempo

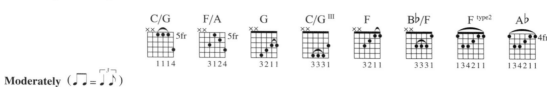

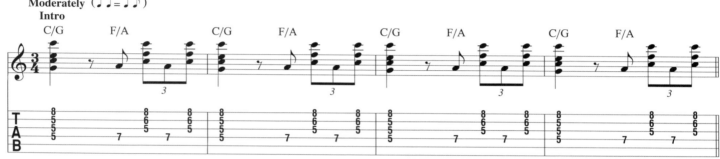

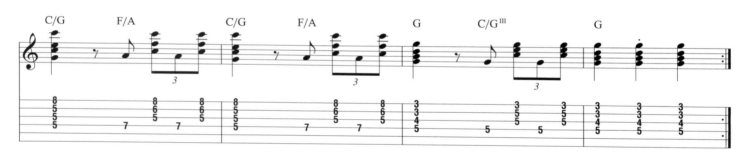

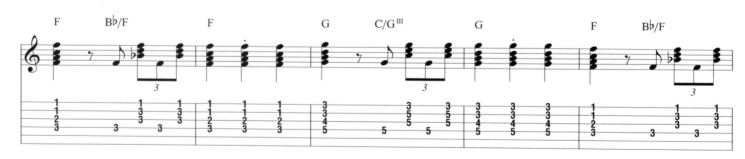

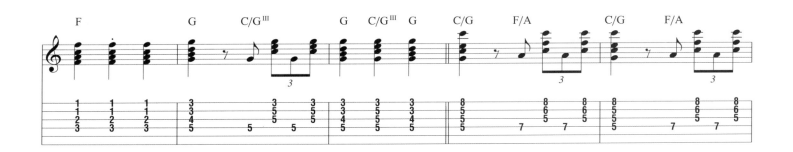

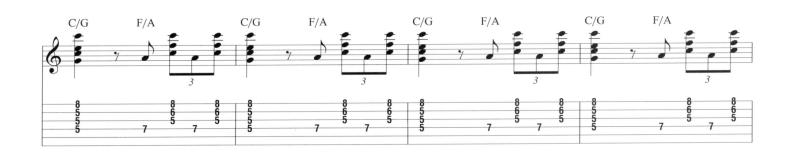

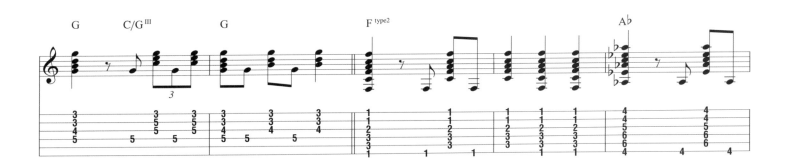

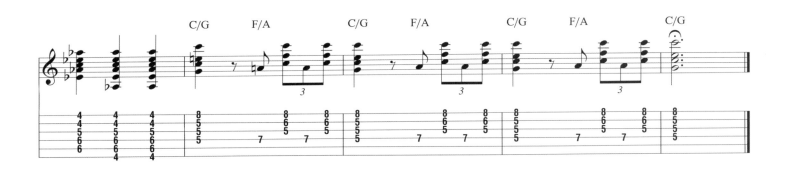

LEAD GUITAR STYLES

This lead guitar part is an accompaniment part as well. It consists of short riffs that are derived from the major pentatonic scales relative to the chord changes, particularly in the B section. But mostly, this part doubles the rhythm guitar for the I–IV–I substitutions via smaller three- and four-note chords.

MOTOR CITY STROLL
Lead

TRACK 28
Slow Tempo

TRACK 29
Full Tempo

"The Gospel Truth" has a gospel feel to it. It begins with a slower, laidback rhythm and moves through a I–IV–V progression. At the end, there is a "cut-time" Coda, where you can pull out the stops and let loose. In *cut-time*, the tempo doubles and the tune moves twice as fast. For example, in 4/4 time, eighth notes become quarter notes. It works like this:

Original time: | 1 & 2 & 3 & 4 & | *becomes...*

Cut-time: | 1 2 3 4 | 1 2 3 4 | (two bars in the same space)

The idea is to generate a lot of excitement.

THE SCALES

In order to create lyrical, melodic lead guitar lines, having a good, working knowledge of arpeggios is very useful. Arpeggios give you a means by which to quickly move across and along the fretboard in large increments, compared to the stepwise motion of scales. You can move two, three, or more steps at a time. Those movements are called *melodic leaps*. Leaps are often what make your melodies more dramatic and interesting. You can arpeggiate any chord. You learned how to do it with partial chords in a simple rhythm guitar part. Now we'll look at some additional arpeggios in the examples below.

Arpeggio Exercise

Note: Play each note individually; do not hold notes as a chord.

continue up by 1/2 steps, then back down the same way...

continue up by 1/2 steps, then back down the same way...

continue up by 1/2 steps, then back down the same way...

(Dominant seventh and minor seventh arpeggios are thoroughly covered in Lessons 9 and 10 of *More Blues You Can Use*.)

THE CHORDS

Another commonly used interval in the R&B guitar style is the 4th, which has a distinctive sound that you'll recognize immediately.

Intervals of a 4th are played on adjacent strings, and the two notes that comprise the interval are positioned on the same fret, with one exception—those found on strings 3 and 2, which are located one fret apart, with the note on string 3 lower than that on string 2.

Like 6ths, 4ths are easiest to work with if you associate them with a chord shape. Below are some possibilities. You should experiment and find more on your own; just be sure to visualize the nearby chord forms.

4th/Chord Relationships
over a G major chord

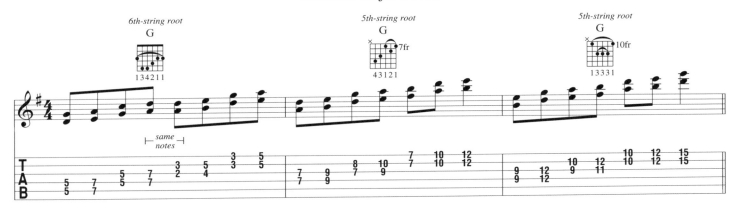

over a C major chord

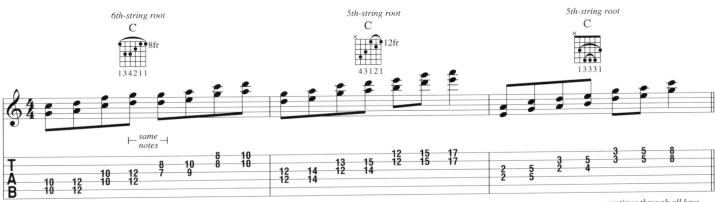

continue through all keys...

Note how the 4ths are related to the notes of the chords and apply those relationships to all of the other keys. The chords move up and down the neck, but the 4ths stay the same, relative to the chord shapes.

Very often, slides are used to connect 4th intervals, which give your lines a smooth, gliding sound. Here is an exercise to help you practice that technique.

Exercise in Sliding 4ths

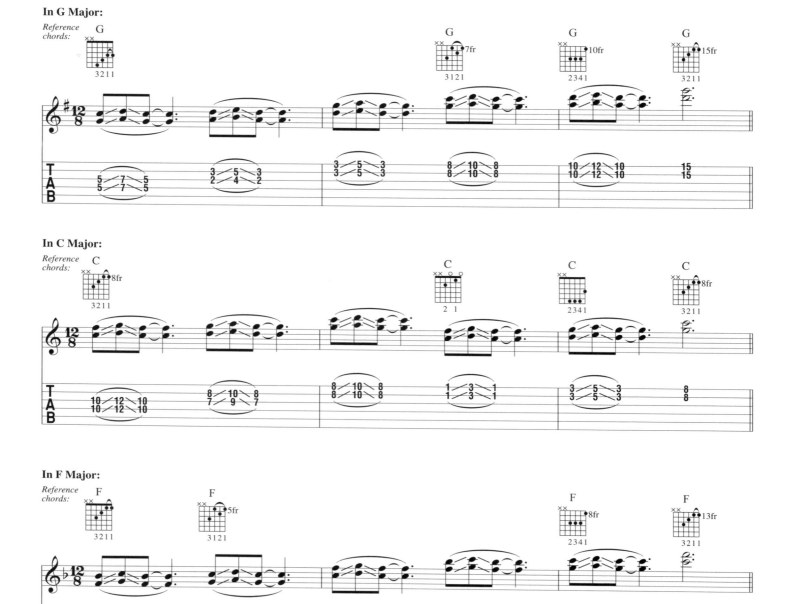

continue through all keys...

RHYTHM GUITAR STYLES

In Lesson 11, you learned the I–IV–I substitution that is so commonly used in R&B. There, major chords were used, with passing IV chords. Now we'll use I7 and I9 chords—dominant seventh types— while still incorporating passing IV chords. The principle is the same. With these new chord shapes, the fingerings become more important. You can use any fingering that you like, but be sure to be consistent with them so you don't get lost or confused. The chord grids were omitted due to all the inversions we are using in this next example.

THE GOSPEL TRUTH

Rhythm

TRACK 30
Slow Tempo

TRACK 31
Full Tempo

LEAD GUITAR STYLES

The lead guitar part to "The Gospel Truth" mixes major pentatonic lines with the 4ths that were introduced earlier in this lesson. The 4ths often are approached with a slide—either up or down to the target. Be sure to use a light touch as you slide. In the Coda, you will play the major chord I–IV–I substitutions that you learned in Lesson 11, which complement the dominant seventh chords of the rhythm guitar part.

THE GOSPEL TRUTH
Lead

TRACK 30
Slow Tempo

TRACK 31
Full Tempo

"Blue Rhythm Sermon," this lesson's study, has a simple 16-bar form that is repeated, as well as an eight-bar intro and a 14-bar Coda. The progression in the main body of the tune, written in the key of F major, is essentially a I–vi–IV–I progression with a I–vi–IV–V tacked on. After repeating the main section, the tune moves to the Coda, which contains a I–V–IV progression that is repeated till the end. Like "Motor City Stroll," "Blue Rhythm Sermon" is written in 3/4 time.

THE SCALES

In the last lesson, you learned major and minor chord arpeggios. Here now are some dominant seventh arpeggios. Although not used much in R&B styles, dominant seventh arpeggios offer a very bluesy/ jazzy sound. I have included dominant ninth chord arpeggios because they have been used in R&B tunes, most notably by James Brown. Remember, you can arpeggiate any chord.

Dominant 7th and 9th Arpeggios

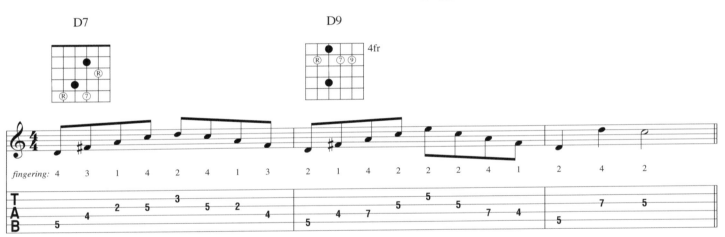

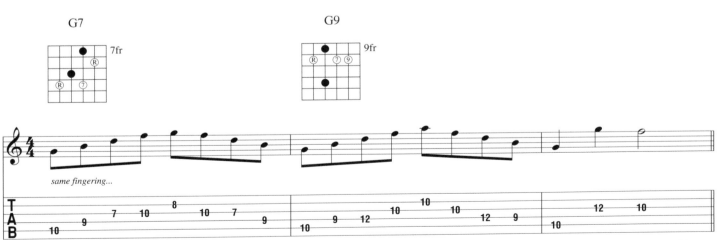

continue through all keys...

THE CHORDS

While the interval of a 3rd is not used all that often in R&B styles, you do hear them. In fact, you played them in the lead guitar part to "Sixties Dance Music," from Lesson 6. Intervals of a 3rd follow the chords in the same way that 6ths and 4ths do. If you invert a 3rd, you get a 6th, retaining the same notes. That is, you take the top note and play it an octave lower, so it is now the bottom note, or you play the bottom note an octave higher, so it is now on top. This is illustrated in *Blues You Can Use*, pages 70–71.

Below are some 3rds, along with their relative chords.

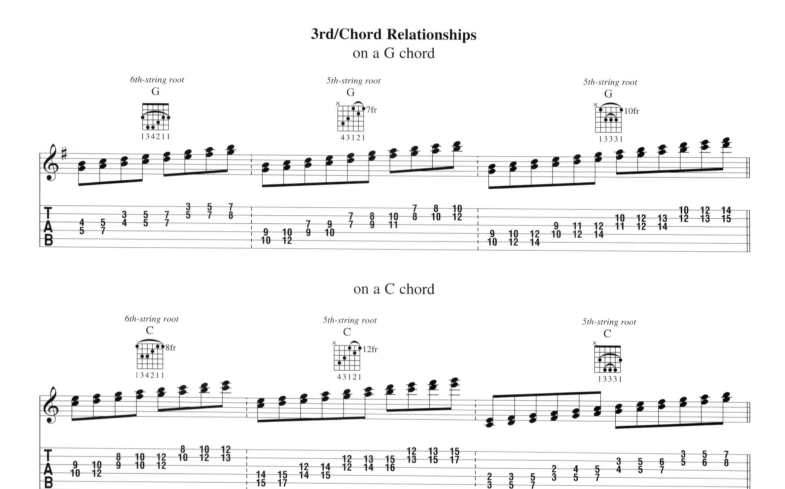

3rd/Chord Relationships
on a G chord

on a C chord

continue through all keys...

RHYTHM GUITAR STYLES

The rhythm guitar part to "Blue Rhythm Sermon" is a very simple chord-chop style, whereby a staccato strum is played on the last beat of every measure. Although played somewhat staccato, let the chords ring briefly before cutting them off. It takes a little practice and a lot of listening, so be patient.

The rhythm part is very simple, so you have a lot of time to think about how to execute the chops.

BLUE RHYTHM SERMON

Rhythm

LEAD GUITAR STYLES

The lead part to "Blue Rhythm Sermon" is actually an active accompaniment part in which you play off the chord shapes, changing the fingerings slightly to incorporate the embellishing/sweetening notes. Chord grids are added in to help you see the connection.

The I–IV–I substitution is present here, but instead of passing between two inversions of the main chord, you simply move up to the IV chord and back down to the I chord.

As always, you may opt to alter the fingerings to something that is more comfortable to you, but be sure to be consistent with them.

BLUE RHYTHM SERMON
Lead

TRACK 32
Slow Tempo

TRACK 33
Full Tempo

In "R&B Stewpot," we explore the beautiful chordal embellishment style that was developed by the masterful guitarists of the "Chitlin' Circuit," passed along by players like Curtis Mayfield, Floyd McDaniel, and Ernie Isley, and crossed over to rock audiences through Jimi Hendrix, who also played on the "Circuit." This style was later picked up by Stevie Ray Vaughan, who used it to great effect in his prettier tunes.

You've already seen how it works in previous lessons. Here, we take it further, making extensive use of the chord/scale relationships explored throughout this book. It's all played over a 16-bar chord progression with a two-bar I (B) chord ending.

THE SCALES

Now we'll look at two final chord arpeggios—minor seventh and minor ninth. They offer a nice, sophisticated, smooth sound. Try to find more on your own.

Minor 7th and Minor 9th Arpeggios

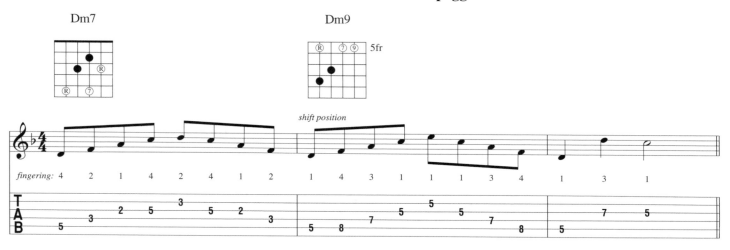

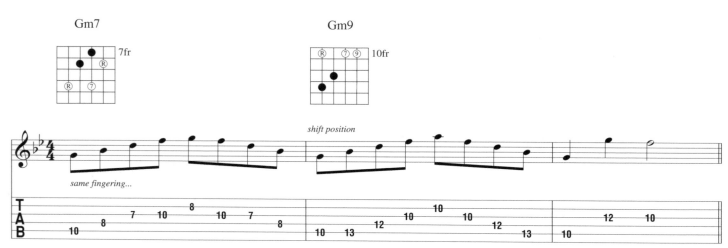

continue through all keys...

THE CHORDS

You have learned the intervals of a 3rd, 4th, and 6th and how to use them, relative to a chord shape. Below is a review of the intervals. After you have learned this exercise, try to create some of your own.

3rds, 4ths, and 6ths Combination Exercise
on a G chord

on a C chord

continue through all keys...

RHYTHM GUITAR STYLES

The rhythm guitar part to "R&B Stewpot" is very, very simple—all you do is play the chord progression in an arpeggiated form, which you've already learned, beginning in Lesson 2. Here though, we play the arpeggios with a staccato feel, cutting short all of the notes of the chords. This approach gives the tune a nice, light feel, with a sensation of "bouncing along" through the progression.

"R&B Stewpot" mostly contains a I–vi–IV–V chord progression (even when the order of the chords varies, no new chords are introduced). Although fairly plain, this rhythmic approach is perfect for providing a solid and completely unobtrusive accompaniment.

R&B STEWPOT

Rhythm

LEAD GUITAR STYLES

The meat of this lesson lies in the lead part to "R&B Stewpot." Mostly using the same chords as those in the rhythm part, embellishing/sweetening notes from the related pentatonic chord/scales are added to create lush chordal movement. A heavy dose of 4ths are used here as well. Chord grids are shown in this arrangement.

The chord/scales are used to create a full, active accompaniment, one that compliments the sparse rhythm guitar part. (The rhythm part is sparse so as to stay out of the way of the lead part.)

R&B STEWPOT

Lead

TRACK 34
Slow Tempo

TRACK 35
Full Tempo

Our last study, "I-Chord Funk," is a simple funk tune that is played entirely on the I chord (G9). Although the arrangement contains some passing chords, it is essentially a one-chord tune.

THE SCALES

Now it's time for you to combine all of the elements that you have learned. In an actual performance, you will do well if they are readily at your disposal. You can accomplish this by practicing them together, in every key. Below is an exercise to help you get started. Once you have worked through it, create your own exercises, using two, three, or even all of the elements.

Chord/Scale/Arpeggio/6ths Combination

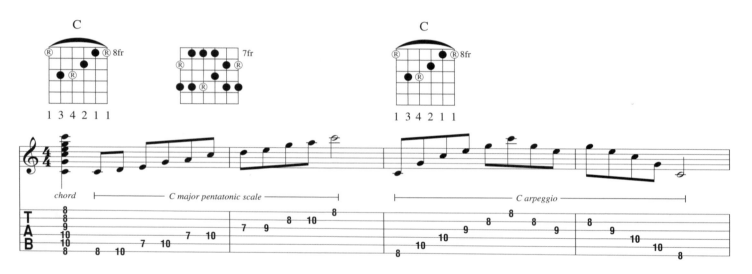

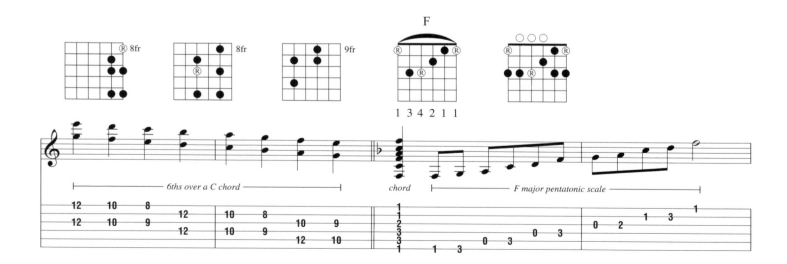

continue through all keys in a similar manner...

THE CHORDS

Now that you have the chords under your fingers and have learned about "sweetening notes" and 4th and 6th intervals, you should begin to create your own chord movements, if you haven't already done so. Remember, most of the embellishments are related to the chords—not the key of the tune—and follow the chords throughout the progression. Here is an exercise to get you started.

Moving Through the Chords in the Key of A Major
(5th-string roots)

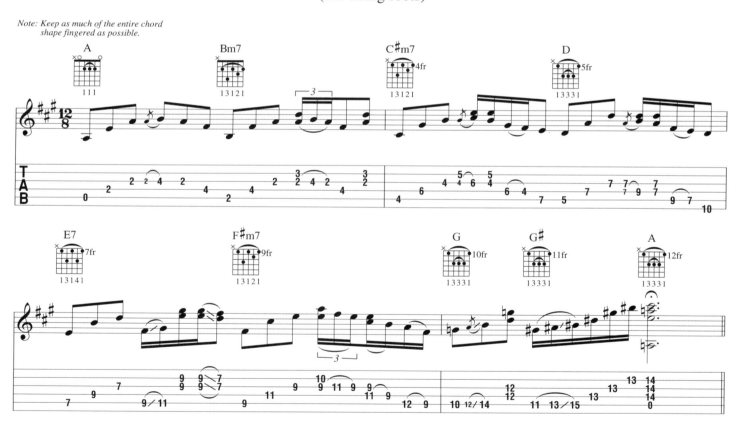

Now make up your own using simple progressions, at least to begin with. You can use any of the progressions in this book or your favorite songs. For example, you can take a rock, folk, or pop song and treat it like an R&B tune. The result will be an R&B version of that tune. It won't always work, but you might be surprised at how often it will.

RHYTHM GUITAR STYLES

This is a heavy, funky, syncopated rhythm part with three basic rhythm patterns, as well as some "hybrids"—combinations of two patterns.

The first pattern is two bars long and found in the first two measures of the tune. It is repeated three times and elsewhere in the tune. You can practice the first two bars to get this pattern down.

The next rhythm pattern is one bar long and first appears in measure 5. Like the first pattern, this one is repeated throughout the tune. Practice measure 5 repeatedly to get this pattern down.

The third rhythm pattern is one bar long and first appears in measures 18–21 (it's repeated four times). This pattern is quite a bit less intense than the first two.

At measure 22, the first pattern is played twice, followed in measure 26 by a one-bar hybrid of the second and first patterns. If you practice measure 26 repeatedly, you'll get this pattern down.

Finally, in measure 30, a shortened version of the hybrid pattern takes you out and ends the tune. Take your time with all of these rhythm patterns.

I-CHORD FUNK
Rhythm

106

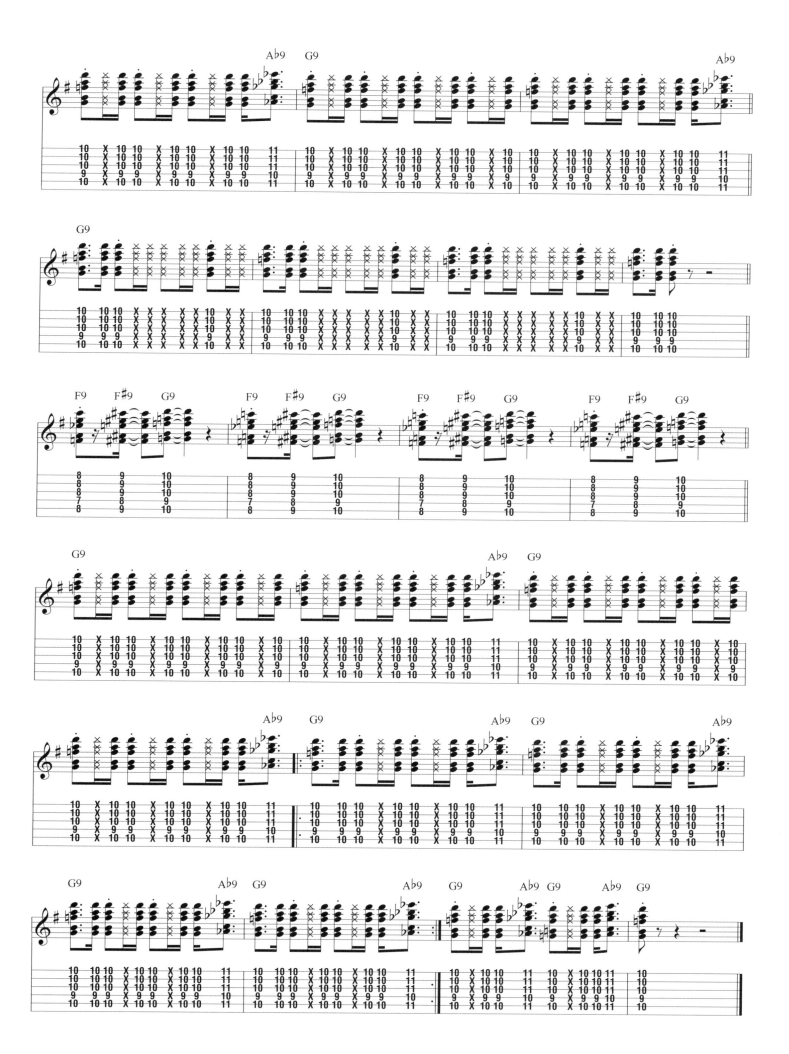

LEAD GUITAR STYLES

The lead guitar part to "I-Chord Funk" is composed of little funky riffs, more for punctuation than melody. The riffs are very short—mostly one-and-a-half or two beats long—and mainly derived from the G minor pentatonic scale.

I-CHORD FUNK
Lead

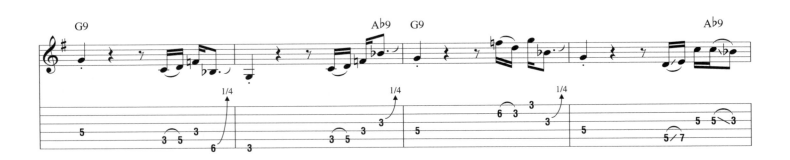

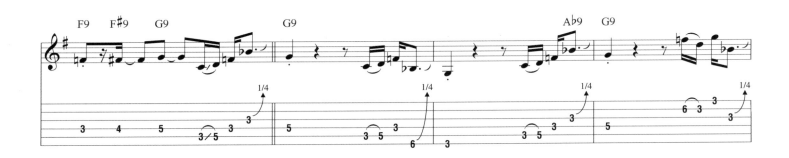
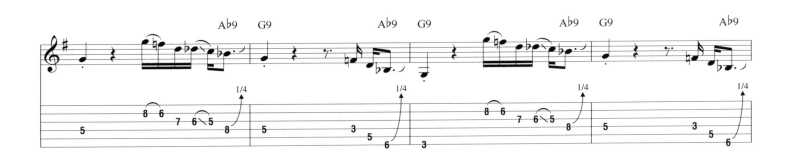
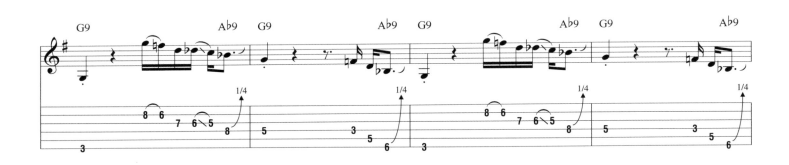
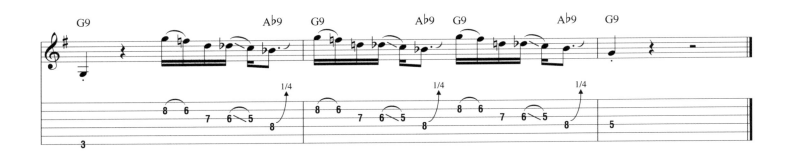

WHERE TO GO FROM HERE

Congratulations on completing the book! If you have no prior experience in these styles, it isn't exactly easy, as you now know. However, by working through this book, you have expanded your knowledge of chords and chord/scales. You have learned about common intervals and how to use them. You have learned new strumming and picking techniques. And, most significantly, you have learned how to play and improvise while following the chord changes, instead of staying in one key. If you continue to work at following the changes and incorporate it into your everyday playing, you'll develop an ability to see where you are in the progression, where you have come from, and where you are headed—all at once! In fact, you probably already can do that to some degree.

So, where do you go to now? You have lots of options. You can continue to study rhythm & blues styles, including the jazzier and more sophisticated areas. You can move into jazz, if you'd like— you've started to learn that theory. For that, I recommend *Jazzin' the Blues*, which I wrote with my good friend and jazz guitar master, David Roos. You can incorporate it into your blues playing. You can stay right where you are and enjoy a lifetime of soulful, rhythmic, and bluesy music. It's your choice.

I do have a few recommendations for everybody, regardless of your inclinations. First, study chord theory—also known as harmony—and expand your abstract and working knowledge of chords. "Abstract" is the theory itself, and "working knowledge" is the ability to find and play any of the chords that you learn on the guitar. You can get a good foundation in chord theory from *Blues You Can Use: Guitar Chords*, an early book in the *Blues You Can Use* series.

Visit my website, *bluesyoucanuse.com*, for updates, corrections (it happens), and supplemental material, as well as information on other books and CDs. You can also communicate and exchange ideas with other blues, jazz, and R&B guitar aficionados in the forum; you can download my guitar arrangements of holiday songs and other tunes; and you can find guest contributors with their own take on guitar study in blues, jazz, and rock styles.

Also, listen to as much music as you can. Listen to Professor Longhair, Allen Toussaint, Fats Domino, Sam Cooke, and Irma Thomas for the New Orleans styles. Listen to Ray Charles for the jazzy/gospel sound. Put on some Aretha Franklin, Otis Redding, Solomon Burke, and anything from the Motown or Atlantic catalogs for the soul music of the '60s. Those artists had great sidemen, including guitarists. As this book was being written, English soul music began to explode, much like the explosion of English blues in the '60s. Take it all in.

Most importantly, at least right now, apply everything that you have learned to anything you might play, whatever the style, including blues, rock, or even some jazz. Keep at it and make it your own. That's how you will retain what you have learned and how you will develop your own style.

Whatever you decide to do, enjoy the journey.

John Ganapes
2013

GUITAR NOTATION LEGEND

Guitar music can be notated three different ways: on a *musical staff*, in *tablature*, and in *rhythm slashes*.

RHYTHM SLASHES are written above the staff. Strum chords in the rhythm indicated. Use the chord diagrams found at the top of the first page of the transcription for the appropriate chord voicings. Round noteheads indicate single notes.

THE MUSICAL STAFF shows pitches and rhythms and is divided by bar lines into measures. Pitches are named after the first seven letters of the alphabet.

TABLATURE graphically represents the guitar fingerboard. Each horizontal line represents a string, and each number represents a fret.

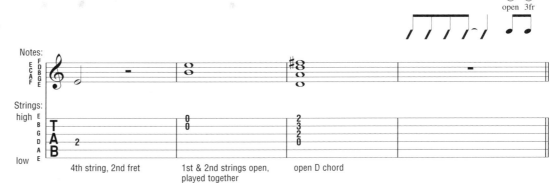

4th string, 2nd fret

1st & 2nd strings open, played together

open D chord

HALF-STEP BEND: Strike the note and bend up 1/2 step.

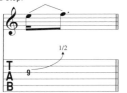

WHOLE-STEP BEND: Strike the note and bend up one step.

GRACE NOTE BEND: Strike the note and immediately bend up as indicated.

SLIGHT (MICROTONE) BEND: Strike the note and bend up 1/4 step.

BEND AND RELEASE: Strike the note and bend up as indicated, then release back to the original note. Only the first note is struck.

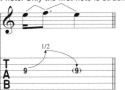

PRE-BEND: Bend the note as indicated, then strike it.

VIBRATO: The string is vibrated by rapidly bending and releasing the note with the fretting hand.

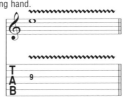

WIDE VIBRATO: The pitch is varied to a greater degree by vibrating with the fretting hand.

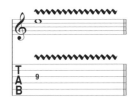

HAMMER-ON: Strike the first (lower) note with one finger, then sound the higher note (on the same string) with another finger by fretting it without picking.

PULL-OFF: Place both fingers on the notes to be sounded. Strike the first note and without picking, pull the finger off to sound the second (lower) note.

LEGATO SLIDE: Strike the first note and then slide the same fret-hand finger up or down to the second note. The second note is not struck.

SHIFT SLIDE: Same as legato slide, except the second note is struck.

TRILL: Very rapidly alternate between the notes indicated by continuously hammering on and pulling off.

TAPPING: Hammer ("tap") the fret indicated with the pick-hand index or middle finger and pull off to the note fretted by the fret hand.

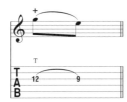

NATURAL HARMONIC: Strike the note while the fret-hand lightly touches the string directly over the fret indicated.

PINCH HARMONIC: The note is fretted normally and a harmonic is produced by adding the edge of the thumb or the tip of the index finger of the pick hand to the normal pick attack.

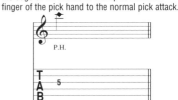

PICK SCRAPE: The edge of the pick is rubbed down (or up) the string, producing a scratchy sound.

MUFFLED STRINGS: A percussive sound is produced by laying the fret hand across the string(s) without depressing, and striking them with the pick hand.

PALM MUTING: The note is partially muted by the pick hand lightly touching the string(s) just before the bridge.

RAKE: Drag the pick across the strings indicated with a single motion.

TREMOLO PICKING: The note is picked as rapidly and continuously as possible.

VIBRATO BAR DIVE AND RETURN: The pitch of the note or chord is dropped a specified number of steps (in rhythm), then returned to the original pitch.

VIBRATO BAR SCOOP: Depress the bar just before striking the note, then quickly release the bar.

VIBRATO BAR DIP: Strike the note and then immediately drop a specified number of steps, then release back to the original pitch.

MASTER the Blues

With guitar instruction from Hal Leonard
All books include notes and tab.

Hal Leonard Guitar Method – Blues Guitar
by Greg Koch

The complete guide to learning blues guitar uses real blues songs to teach you the basics of rhythm and lead blues guitar in the style of B.B. King, Buddy Guy, Eric Clapton, and many others. Lessons include: 12-bar blues; chords, scales and licks; vibrato and string bending; riffs, turnarounds, and boogie patterns; and more!
00697326 Book/CD Pack $16.99

Blues Deluxe
by Dave Rubin

Not only does this deluxe edition provide accurate transcriptions of ten blues classics plus performance notes and artist bios, it also includes a CD with the *original Alligator Records recordings* of every song! Tunes: Are You Losing Your Mind? (Buddy Guy) • Don't Take Advantage of Me (Johnny Winter) • Gravel Road (Magic Slim) • Somebody Loan Me a Dime (Fenton Robinson) • and more.
00699918 Book/CD Pack $24.99

Art of the Shuffle
by Dave Rubin

This method book explores shuffle, boogie and swing rhythms for guitar. Includes tab and notation, and covers Delta, country, Chicago, Kansas City, Texas, New Orleans, West Coast, and bebop blues. Also includes audio for demonstration of each style and to jam along with.
00695005 Book/CD Pack $19.95

Power Trio Blues
by Dave Rubin

This book/CD pack details how to play electric guitar in a trio with bass and drums. Boogie, shuffle, and slow blues rhythms, licks, double stops, chords, and bass patterns are presented for full and exciting blues. A CD with the music examples performed by a smokin' power trio is included for play-along instruction and jamming.
00695028 Book/CD Pack $19.99

100 Blues Lessons
Guitar Lesson Goldmine
by John Heussenstamm and Chad Johnson

A huge variety of blues guitar styles and techniques are covered, including: turnarounds, hammer-ons and pull-offs, slides, the blues scale, 12-bar blues, double stops, muting techniques, hybrid picking, fingerstyle blues, and much more!
00696452 Book/2-CD Pack $24.99

Electric Slide Guitar
by David Hamburger

This book/audio method explores the basic fundamentals of slide guitar: from selecting a slide and proper setup of the guitar, to open and standard tuning. Plenty of music examples are presented showing sample licks as well as backup/rhythm slide work. Each section also examines techniques and solos in the style of the best slide guitarists, including Duane Allman, Dave Hole, Ry Cooder, Bonnie Raitt, Muddy Waters, Johnny Winter and Elmore James.
00695022 Book/CD Pack $19.95

101 Must-Know Blues Licks
A Quick, Easy Reference for All Guitarists
by Wolf Marshall

Now you can add authentic blues feel and flavor to your playing! Here are 101 definitive licks – plus a demonstration CD – from every major blues guitar style, neatly organized into easy-to-use categories. They're all here, including Delta blues, jump blues, country blues, Memphis blues, Texas blues, West Coast blues, Chicago blues, and British blues.
00695318 Book/CD Pack $17.95

Fretboard Roadmaps Blues Guitar
for Acoustic and Electric Guitar
by Fred Sokolow

These essential fretboard patterns are roadmaps that all great blues guitarists know and use. This book teaches how to: play lead and rhythm anywhere on the fretboard, in any key; play a variety of lead guitar styles; play chords and progressions anywhere on the fretboard, in any key; expand chord vocabulary; learn to think musicially, the way the pros do.
00695350 Book/CD Pack $14.95

The Road to Robert Johnson
The Genesis and Evolution of Blues in the Delta from the Late 1800s Through 1938
by Edward Komara

This book traces the development of the legendary Robert Johnson's music in light of the people and songs that directly and indirectly influenced him. It includes much information about life in the Delta from the late 1800s to Johnson's controversial death in 1938, and features fascinating historical photos, maps, musical examples and much more.
00695388 .... $14.95

12-Bar Blues
by Dave Rubin

The term "12-bar blues" has become synonymous with blues music and is the basis for an incredible body of jazz, rock 'n' roll, and other forms of popular music. This book/CD pack is solely devoted to providing guitarists with all the technical tools necessary for playing 12-bar blues with authority. The CD includes 24 full-band tracks. Covers: boogie, shuffle, swing, riff, and jazzy blues progressions; Chicago, minor, slow, bebop, and other blues styles; soloing, intros, turnarounds, and more.
00695187 Book/CD Pack $18.99

Smokin' Blues Guitar
by Smokin' Joe Kubek with Dave Rubin

Texas blues guitar legend Smokin' Joe Kubek and acclaimed author and music historian Dave Rubin have teamed up to create this one-of-a-kind DVD/book bundle, featuring a high-definition DVD with Smokin' Joe himself demonstrating loads of electric blues licks, riffs, concepts, and techniques straight from his extensive arsenal. The companion book, co-written with Dave Rubin, provides standard notation and tablature for every smokin' example on the DVD, as well as bonus instructional material, and much more!
00696469 Book/DVD Pack $24.99

Blues You Can Use
by John Ganapes

A comprehensive source for learning blues guitar, designed to develop both your lead and rhythm playing. Covers all styles of blues, including Texas, Delta, R&B, early rock and roll, gospel, blues/rock and more. Includes 21 complete solos; extensive instruction; audio with leads and full band backing; and more!
00695007 Book/CD Pack $19.99

Blues You Can Use Chord Book
by John Ganapes

A reference guide to blues, R&B, jazz, and rock rhythm guitar, with hundreds of voicings, chord theory construction, chord progressions and exercises and much more. The Blues You Can Use Book Of Guitar Chords is useful for the beginner to advanced player.
00695082 .... $14.95

More Blues You Can Use
by John Ganapes

A complete guide to learning blues guitar, covering scales, rhythms, chords, patterns, rakes, techniques, and more. CD includes 13 full-demo solos.
00695165 Book/CD Pack $19.95

Blues Licks You Can Use
by John Ganapes

Contains music and performance notes for 75 hot lead phrases, covering styles including up-tempo and slow blues, jazz-blues, shuffle blues, swing blues and more! CD features full-band examples.
00695386 Book/CD Pack $16.95

HAL•LEONARD®
CORPORATION

7777 W. BLUEMOUND RD. P.O. BOX 13819 MILWAUKEE, WI 53213

www.halleonard.com

Prices, availability, and contents subject to change without notice. Some products may not be available outside the U.S.A.

0313